THE

SAINTS

PRAYER BOOK

THE

SAINTS

PRAYER BOOK

Compiled by
Anthony F. Chiffolo

CANTERBURY
PRESS
Norwich

To my daughter, Lisa

First published in the USA by Ligouri Publications

First published in the UK in 1998 by
The Canterbury Press Norwich (a publishing imprint
of Hymns Ancient & Modern Limited
a registered charity)
St Mary's Works, St Mary's Plain
Norwich, Norfolk, NR3 3BH

British Library Cataloguing in Publication Data

A catalogue record for this book is available
from the British Library

ISBN 1-85311-230-5

Printed and bound in Great Britain by
Biddles Ltd, Guildford and King's Lynn

O Holy Spirit, grant me the gift of prayer.
Come into my heart, and teach me the strength not to
    abandon it because I sometimes grow weary of it;
And give me the spirit of prayer, the grace to pray
    continually.

St. Alphonsus de' Liguori

CONTENTS

INTRODUCTION

I've been praying ever since I can remember, though I would not say that I'm a mighty prayer warrior, nor even a mediocre prayer. Although for much of my life I relied on rote prayers, most of my praying of late is strictly conversational—telling God what's happening in my life and how I feel about it all. Praying in this way connects me with God—who might sometimes seem inaccessible, but who is always listening when I cry out in yearning or sorrow or exaltation. My greatest need is to establish a relationship with the divine, and this I cannot do unless and until I speak to God. And that to me is the definition of prayer: speaking to God out of the depths of my true being.

St Alphonsus de' Liguori, who is sometimes called the Great Doctor of Prayer, summarized the essence of prayer in this way:

> Acquire the habit of speaking to God as if you were alone with him. Speak with familiarity and confidence as to your dearest and most loving friend. Speak of your life, your plans, your troubles, your joys, your fears. In return, God will speak to you—not that you will hear audible words in your ears, but words that you will clearly understand in your heart. These may be feelings of peace, hope, interior joy, or sorrow for sin…gentle knockings at the door of your heart.

God speaks to us constantly, in ways both subtle and obvious, through the people we encounter, the news, the weather, or even the state of our health, but we will not be tuned in to God's message unless and until we begin to converse with him. The saints knew this and spoke to him with absolute truthfulness, baring their desires and failings and proclaiming their thanksgiving and adoration, as the prayers in this collection show so well. Indeed, sanctity seems to be linked with the ability to tune in to God, for to be able to integrate his will with our own, we must first be able to hear him speaking to us within the depths of our being.

Real prayer is an ongoing dialogue with God, but this spontaneous two-way conversation does not come naturally to most people. Just as we might stumble in our first attempts to communicate with new friends or colleagues, we might also need to practise talking with God. We might feel awkward or foolish at first in speaking aloud to God, in telling God how afraid we might be about moving to a new home or how distressed we are about a relationship gone awry, but God will touch our hearts when we pray with sincerity, and we will soon find that we have been given the grace not only to speak to God as a friend but also to deal with the realities that face us.

A brief word about the four categories of prayers: adoration, sorrow, petition, and thanksgiving. These are the categories recommended by St Alphonsus, although in his own prayers he often combined the types, starting with words of adoration and progressing through expressions of sorrow, petitions, and finally heartfelt thanks. Indeed, in prayer as in many other conversations, we might not at first know what to say: our emotions might be mixed up and our desires unclear. So we may start out thanking God for today's blessings but end up entreating God for a solution to a thorny family problem. Perhaps a measure of our honesty in talking with God is whether our prayers enable us to express our true needs and reveal the desires of our heart, even if the way is roundabout. If so, the prayers in this collection are transparently honest, for the saints themselves mix entreaties in with their praises. This makes any categorizing difficult and somewhat arbitrary. And the greater number of petitionary prayers, compared with the number of prayers of the other types, indicates that the saints, like all the rest of us, felt compelled to cry out to God in need. Indeed, St Alphonsus highly recommended that all prayer include earnest petitions for needed graces, including forgiveness for transgressions, perfect love of God, and a happy death.

Following that recommendation, as we learn to open our hearts to God, we might find it easier to concentrate on asking him for whatever it is we desire, as our requests usually come to mind first. But complete honesty in this regard should soon lead us to speak with him about all of our experiences. We will find ourselves easily talking to God about our regrets, thanking him for the blessings we have received, and praising him for the graces that we experience entering into our lives as a result of openness in prayer. The results of such honest communication with him will be precious—and astonishing.

Having communicated openly with God, many of the saints themselves were astonished with the results of their prayers, for they were often led in ways that they had never imagined. This could have been terrifying—indeed, it is for most people—but once a prayer-life had grown, once a connection with God had been established, there was no fear, no mistrusting the paths that were opening up. And in the case of the saints, these paths led to what can only be called a miraculous diversity of graces. It is my heartfelt hope that the prayers in this collection will serve as examples of trust, preparing the reader to speak to God as a friend, to listen to God's responses, and to follow wherever he leads.

PRAYERS
OF
ADORATION

God, our most loyal friend,
In all the ideals that love can blend
You are our all, you are our end.
Bd Ramón Lull

Let your voice sound in my ears, good Jesus, that I may learn how my heart, my mind, my soul can love you. The inmost recesses of my heart embrace you, my one and only true good, my sweet and delectable joy.

St Aelred of Rievaulx

O Lord, my creator, from my birth you have always protected me; you have taken from me the love of the world and given me patience to suffer. Receive now my soul.

St Agatha

O my Jesus, draw me entirely to you. Draw me with all the love of my heart. If I knew that one fibre of my heart did not palpitate for you, I would tear it out at any cost. But I know that I could not speak without your help. Draw me, O my Jesus, draw me completely. I know it well, my heart cannot rest until it rests in your heart.

Bd Aloysius Guanella

O God of life, I love you more than myself. You alone are enough for me. I consecrate to you all my love. Since you have drawn me to that love, I leave all, I renounce all, and I bind myself to you.

St Alphonsus de' Liguori

O my God, you have treated us with so much love. Help us to realize what a great good you really are. Never allow us to forget your goodness and love.

St Alphonsus de' Liguori

My most sweet Lord, I offer and consecrate to you this morning all that I am and have: my senses, my thoughts, my affections, my desires, my pleasures, my inclinations, my liberty. In a word, I place my whole body and soul in your hands.

St Alphonsus de' Liguori

O my God, why have you loved me so much? What good do you find in me? Have you forgotten my sins and offences? Since you have treated me with so much love, and given me graces without number, I will love you from now on, my God and my all, with all my heart. You alone are and always will be the God of my heart, my only good, my heaven, my hope, my all.

St Alphonsus de' Liguori

God, eternal truth,
We believe in you.

God, our strength and salvation,
We hope in you.

God, infinite goodness,
We love you with our whole heart.

You have sent your Son as Saviour of the world,
Let us all be one in him.

Send us the Spirit of your Son,
That we may glorify your name in all things. Amen.

Bd Arnold Janssen

Every beat of my heart
Every breath of my mouth
Take as an act of love
And bind us all with you,
O holy and triune God.

Bd Arnold Janssen

O Holy Spirit, I desire to serve you with a wholehearted love
and single-minded intention, and to love you in union with
Mary, St Joseph, and all your saints. I unite my poor offering
with the love they have for you and with which they will
adore, praise, and revere you together with your Son for all
eternity. Amen.

Bd Arnold Janssen

O holy, triune God, I consecrate my memory to God the
Father so that it may seek its rest in its Creator and not in
creatures. I consecrate my understanding to God the Son so
that he may penetrate it with his light. I consecrate my heart
and will to God the Holy Spirit so that he may regulate all our
affections and perfect them through his love. Amen.

Bd Arnold Janssen

...You, Lord, are always at work, and are always at rest. You
do not see in time, nor are you moved in time, nor do you rest
in time; and yet you make things seen in time, even the times
themselves, and the rest that results from time.

We, therefore, see these things that you made, because they
are: but they are because you see them. And we see without,

that they are, and within that they are good, but you saw them there, when made, where you saw them, yet to be made. And we were at a later time moved to do well, after our hearts had conceived of your Spirit; but in the former time we were moved to do evil, forsaking you; but you, the One, the good God, never ceased doing good. And we also have some good works, of your gift, but not eternal; after them we trust to rest in your great blessing. But you, being the Good needing no good, are ever at rest, because your rest is you yourself. And what man can teach man to understand this? or what angel, an angel? or what angel, a man? Let it be asked of you, sought in you, knocked for at you; so, so shall it be received, so shall it be found, so shall it be opened. Amen.

St Augustine

O Jesus! Jesus!
  No longer do I feel my cross, when now I think of yours!
St Bernadette Soubirous of Lourdes

You, therefore, God the Father,
  by whom as Creator we live;
You, Wisdom of the Father,
  by whom we have been redeemed and guided
    to live wisely;
You, Holy Spirit, object of our love,
  source of our affections,
We so dwell and yet look forward to
    live more so.

Eternal Trinity, one in substance,
the One God,
    from whom we are,
    by whom we are,
    in whom we are,
Sin has taken us far from you,
Sin has deformed our image of you,
Yet you do not wish us to perish.

To you we return, as the beginning,
To you, the pattern that we are following,
To you, the grace by which we are reconciled,
    we adore you!
    we bless you!
To you be the glory for ever and ever, Amen.

St Bernard of Clairvaux

Rightly so, O Lord Jesus, has my heart declared to you: 'My face has sought you; your face, Lord, will I seek' (Psalm 27:8). You enabled me to hear your mercy in the morning when I lay prone in the dust, kissing the prints of your sacred steps; for you did pardon the evil of my former life. Then as the day of my life went on, you have rejoiced the soul of your servant. Since by the kiss of your hand, you accorded to me the grace to live well. And now what remains, O good Lord, is to admit me into the fullness of your light, in fervour of my spirit, to kiss your divine lips. You have fulfilled from within me the joy of your countenance.

St Bernard of Clairvaux

Jesus! How sweet is the very thought of him, giving true joy to the heart; but surpassing honey and all sweetness in his own presence.

Nothing more sweet can be proclaimed, nothing more pleasant can be heard, nothing more loving can be thought of than Jesus, the Son of God.

O Jesus, the hope of penitents, how kind you are to those who pray. How good to those who seek you—but what to those who find!

No tongue can tell, nor can the written word express it: only one who knows from experience can say what it means to love Jesus.

May you, O Jesus, be our joy as you will be our reward. In you be our glory forever.

St Bernard of Clairvaux

Jesus, name full of glory, grace, love, and strength! You are the refuge of those who repent, our banner of warfare in this life, the medicine of souls, the comfort of those who mourn, the delight of those who believe, the light of those who preach the true faith, the wages of those who toil, the healing of the sick.

To you our devotion aspires; by you our prayers are received; we delight in contemplating you. O name of Jesus, you are the glory of all the saints for eternity. Amen.

St Bernardine of Siena

Eternal praise to you, my Lord Jesus Christ, for the time you endured on the cross the greatest torments and sufferings for us sinners. The sharp pain of your wounds fiercely penetrated even to your blessed soul and cruelly pierced your most sacred heart till finally you sent forth your spirit in peace, bowed your head and humbly commended yourself into the hands of God your Father, and your whole body remained cold in death.

Blessed may you be, my Lord Jesus Christ. For our salvation you allowed your side and heart to be pierced with a lance and from that side water and your precious blood flowed out abundantly for our redemption.

Unending honour be to you, my Lord Jesus Christ. On the third day you rose from the dead and appeared to those you had chosen. And after forty days you ascended into heaven before the eyes of many witnesses and then in heaven you gathered together in glory those you love, whom you had freed from hell.

Rejoicing and eternal praise be to you, my Lord Jesus Christ, who sent the Holy Spirit into the hearts of your disciples and increased the boundless love of God in their spirits. Blessed are you and praiseworthy and glorious forever, my Lord Jesus.

St Birgitta

Blessed are you, O my God, my Creator and Redeemer. You are the ransom by which we have been redeemed from captivity, by which we are directed to all salutary things, by which we are associated to the Unity and Trinity. If I blush for my own sloth, yet I rejoice, that you who died once for our salvation will die no more. For you are truly he that was before the ages. You are he that has power of life and death. You alone are good and just. You alone are almighty and fearful. May you be blessed forever.

St Birgitta

O tender Love, I want all of you. I could not live if I thought I were to do without even a spark of you.

St Catherine of Genoa

O sweetest Jesus! Son of God and of the Virgin Mary!

St Catherine of Siena

O Jesus, you are my true friend, my only friend. You take a part in all my misfortunes; you take them upon yourself; you know how to change them into blessings.

You listen to me with the greatest kindness when I relate my troubles to you, and you always have balm to pour on my wounds. I find you at all times; I find you everywhere; you never go away; if I have to change my dwelling, I find you wherever I go.

You never weary of listening to me; you are never tired of doing me good. I am certain of being loved by you if I love you; my goods are nothing to you, and by bestowing yours on me, you never grow poor. However miserable I may be, no one more noble or learned or even holier can come between you and me and deprive me of your friendship; and death, which tears us away from all other friends, will unite me to you forever.

All the humiliations attached to old age, or to loss of honour, will never detach me from you. On the contrary, I shall never enjoy you more fully, and you will never be closer to me than when everything seems to conspire against me, to overwhelm me and to cast me down.

You bear with all my faults with extreme patience. Even my want of fidelity and my ingratitude do not wound you to such

a degree as to make you unwilling to receive me back when I
return to you. O Jesus! Grant that I may die praising you, that
I may die loving you; that I may die for love of you. Amen.

St Claude de la Colombière

What God wants, as God wants, and when God wants.

St Clement Maria Hofbauer

Jesus, I want to live as long as you will; I want to suffer as you
will me to; I want to die as soon as you will it.

St Clement Maria Hofbauer

I

Who are you, sweet light that fills me
And illumines the darkness of my heart?
You guide me like a mother's hand,
And if you let me go, I could not take
Another step.
You are the space
That surrounds and contains my being.
Without you it would sink into the abyss
Of nothingness from which you raised it into being.
You, closer to me than I to myself,
More inward than my innermost being—
And yet unreachable, untouchable,
And bursting the confines of any name:
    Holy Spirit—
        Eternal love!

II

Are you not the sweet manna
Which flows from the heart of the Son
    Into mine,
Food for angels and for the blessed?
He who from death to life arose,
Has awakened me, too, to new life,
From the sleep of death,
New life he gives me day by day.
Some day his abundance will completely flow through me,
Life of your life—yes, you yourself:
    Holy Spirit—
        Eternal life!

III

Are you the ray
That flashes from the eternal Judge's throne
To pierce into the night of my soul,
Which never knew itself?
Merciful, yet unrelenting, it penetrates the hidden crevices.
The soul takes fright at sight of her own self,
Makes room for holy awe,
For the beginning of that wisdom
Descending from on high,
And anchoring us securely in the heights,—
For your workings, which create us anew:
    Holy Spirit—
        All-penetrating ray!

IV

Are you the wealth of spirit and of power
By which the Lamb loosens the seals
From God's eternal decree?
Driven by you the messengers of judgment
Ride through the world
And with sharp sword divide
The reign of light from the reign of night.
Then the heavens are renewed, and new the earth,
And through your breath
Everything finds its rightful place:
    Holy Spirit—
        Conquering power!

V

Are you the master who builds the eternal dome
Rising from earth and through to very heaven?
The columns, enlivened by you, rise high
And stand firm, immovable.
Marked with the eternal name of God,
They reach high up into the light,
Bearing the cupola, which crowns the holy dome,
Your work encompassing the universe,
    Holy Spirit—
        God's shaping hand.

VI

Are you the one who made the mirror bright,
Which stands beside the throne of the Almighty
Just like a sea of crystal

Wherein the Godhead views himself with love?
You bend over the most marvellous of your creations
And beaming shines your splendour back to you.
The pure beauty of all beings
United in the lovely form of
The virgin, your flawless bride:
   Holy Spirit—
      Creator of the world.

VII

Are you the sweet song of love, and of holy awe,
Resounding ever round God's throne triune,
Which unifies the pure tone of all beings,
Within itself?
The harmony which fits the limbs to the head,
So that each blissfully finds the secret meaning
Of his being,
And exudes it with gladness freely dissolved
In your streams:
   Holy Spirit—
      Eternal jubilation!

Bd Edith Stein

My God, well may I cling to you—for whom have I in heaven
but you? And who upon earth besides you, my heart and my
portion forever?

St Elizabeth Ann Bayley Seton

Holy Spirit, goodness, supreme beauty!
O you whom I adore, O you whom I love!
Consume with your divine flames
This body and this heart and this soul!
This spouse of the Trinity
Who desires only your will!

Bd Elizabeth of the Trinity

May your grace bring me also back,
    who am held in captivity;
my forefathers were taken away captive
    from the Garden of Eden
to this land of thorns
    through Satan's ill counsel;
it was he who has beguiled me
    into dearly loving
this land of curses,
    this place of chastisement.
Blessed is he who has brought us back from captivity
    and slain him who took us away captive.

St Ephrem the Syrian

Lord, I seek little of this world's wealth. If I may only be
allowed to live and serve you, I would be content. If, however,
this seems too much in the eyes of those who persecute me, I
am willing to give up my life before I forsake my faith.

St Ferreolus of Vienne

Lord, you have made me touch almost tangibly that you are
the one who acts, that you are the one who has done
everything, and that I am not even an instrument in your
hands, as others say. You alone are the one who does all, and I
am nothing more than a spectator of the great and beautiful
works which you know how to accomplish.

St Frances Cabrini

O God, thou art the object of my love;
Not for the hope of endless joys above,
Nor for the fear of endless pains below,
Which those who love you not must undergo.

For me and such as me, thou once didst bear
The ignominious cross, the nails, the spear:
A thorny crown did pierce thy sacred brow;
And bloody sweats from every member flow.

Such as then was and is thy love for me,
Such is and shall be still my love for thee;
Thy love, O Jesus, will I ever sing—
O God of love, sweet Saviour, dearest King!

St Francis Xavier

O God: you are my God: in you will I hope! You will be my
help and my refuge: I shall not fear, for not only are you with
me, but you are in me and I in you. Amen.

St Francis de Sales

We adore you, Lord Jesus Christ, here and in all your churches in the whole world, and we bless you because by your holy cross you have redeemed the world.

St Francis of Assisi

Almighty, most holy, most high, and supreme God, highest good, all good, wholly good, who alone are good. To you we render all praise, all glory, all thanks, all honour, all blessing, and we shall always refer all good to you. Amen.

St Francis of Assisi

You are holy, Lord God, who alone work wonders. You are strong. You are great. You are most high. You are the almighty King, you, holy Father, King of heaven and earth. You are the Lord God triune and one; all good. You are good, all good, highest good, Lord God living and true. You are charity, love. You are wisdom. You are humility. You are patience. You are security. You are quietude. You are joy and gladness. You are justice and temperance. You are all riches to sufficiency. You are beauty. You are meekness. You are protector. You are guardian and defender. You are strength. You are refreshment. You are our hope. You are our faith. You are our great sweetness. You are our eternal life, great and admirable Lord, God almighty, merciful Saviour.

St Francis of Assisi

Most high, omnipotent, good Lord,
Praise, glory, honour, and benediction—all are yours.
To you alone do they belong, Most High,
And there is no one fit to mention you.

Praise be to you, my Lord, with all your creatures,
Especially to my worshipful brother sun,
Who lights up the day, and through him do you give brightness;
And beautiful is he and radiant with great splendour;
Most High, he represents you to us.

Praised be my Lord for sister moon and for the stars,
In heaven you have formed them clear and precious and fair.

Praised be my Lord for brother wind
And for the air and clouds and fair and every kind of weather,
By whom you give to your creatures nourishment.
Praised be my Lord for sister water,
Who is greatly helpful and humble and precious and pure.

Praised be my Lord for brother fire,
By whom you light up the dark.
And fair is he and gay and mighty and strong.

Praised be my Lord for our sister, mother earth,
Who sustains and keeps us
And brings forth diverse fruits with grass and flowers bright.

Praised be my Lord for those who for your love forgive
And bear weakness and tribulation.
Blessed those who shall in peace endure,
For by you, Most High, shall they be crowned.

Praised be my Lord for our sister the bodily death,
From whom no living person can flee.
Woe to them who die in mortal sin;
Blessed those who shall find themselves in your most holy will,
For the second death shall do them no ill.

Praise you and bless you, my Lord, and give him thanks,
And be subject to him with great humility.

St Francis of Assisi

Praise to the unbounded love of Jesus, who, moved to pity by
my misery, offers me every means of coming to his love! You,
Jesus, are a treasure not known to me before; but now, Jesus, I
have known you. You are all mine, especially your heart. Yes,
your heart is mine because you have so often given it to me.
But your heart, Jesus, is full of light, and mine is full of
darkness. When, O when shall I pass from this darkness to
that clear light of my Jesus?

But how shall I be able, my God, to praise you? When you
created me, you made me without me; so likewise even
without me you have the praise you deserve. Then let all your
works, made from the sublimity of your majesty, praise you.
My mind has beginning and end; but the praise that God
possesses shall never have an end; and when we praise you, O
Lord, it is not we, it is you who praises yourself in yourself.

St Gemma Galgani

Great God! How I love you, O how I love you!

St Gemma Galgani

O most noble balsam of the Divinity, pouring yourself out like an ocean of charity, shooting forth and budding eternally, diffusing yourself until the end of time! O invincible strength of the hand of the Most High, which causes so frail a vessel, and one that should be cast away in contempt, to receive within it so precious a liquor! O evident testimony of the exuberance of divine goodness, not to withdraw from me when I wandered in the devious ways of sin, but rather to unite me to itself as far as my misery would permit!

St Gertrude of Helfta

O ardent fire of my God, which contains, produces, and imprints those living ardours that attract the humid waters of my soul, and dry up the torrents of earthly delights, and afterward soften my hard self-opinionatedness, which time has hardened so exceedingly! O consuming fire, which even amid ardent flames imparts sweetness and peace to the soul! In you, and in none other, do we receive this grace of being reformed to the image and likeness in which we were created. O burning furnace, in which we enjoy the true vision of peace, which tries and purifies the gold of the elect, and leads the soul to seek eagerly for its highest good, even yourself, in your eternal truth.

St Gertrude of Helfta

What, my Beloved, O realization of all my desires, what, my beloved Lord, should I say to you while I am struck dumb with love? My heart is full of loving thoughts, if only my tongue could express them! What I experience is bottomless;

what I love is endless; and, therefore, what I want to say is
wordless. You are my King, you are my Lord, you are my love,
you are my joy, you are my hour of gladness.

Bd Henry Suso

Strength of the everlasting!
In your heart you invented
order.

Then you spoke the word and
all that you ordered was,
just as you wished.
And your word put on vestments
woven of flesh
cut from a woman
born of Adam
to bleach the agony out of his clothes.

The Saviour is grand and kind!
from the breath of God he took flesh
unfettered
(for sin was not in it)
to set everything free
and bleach the agony out of his clothes.

Glorify the Father,
The Spirit and the Son.

He bleached the agony out of his clothes.

St Hildegard of Bingen

O handiwork of God,
O human form divine!
In great holiness
you were fashioned,
for the Holy One pierced the heavens
in great humility
and the splendour of God shone forth
in the slime of the earth:
the angels that minister on high
see heaven clothed in humanity.

St Hildegard of Bingen

Blessed be the God and Father of our Lord Jesus Christ, who
of his great and abundant goodness willed that I should be a
partaker of the sufferings of his Christ and a true and faithful
witness of his divinity.

St Ignatius of Antioch

Here I am, O supreme King and Lord of all things, I, so
unworthy, but still confiding in your grace and help, I offer
myself entirely to you and submit all that is mine to your will.
In the presence of your infinite goodness, and under the sight
of your glorious Virgin Mother and of the whole heavenly
court, I declare that this is my intention, my desire, and my
firm decision: Provided it will be for your greatest praise and
for my best obedience to you, to follow you as nearly as
possible, and to imitate you in bearing injustices and
adversities, with true poverty, of spirit and things as well, if [I
say] it pleases your holiest Majesty to elect and accept me for
such a state of life.

St Ignatius of Loyola

We also with these blessed powers, Lord and lover of men, cry and say, holy are you and all holy, you and your only-begotten Son, and your Holy Spirit. Holy are you and all holy, and great is the majesty of your glory....

St John Chrysostom

Eternal God, behold me prostrate before your immense majesty, humbly adoring you. I offer you all my thoughts, words, and actions of this day.

I offer them all to be thought, spoken, and done entirely for love of you, for your glory, to fulfil your divine will, to serve you, to praise you and bless you....

I wish and intend to do everything in union with the most pure intentions of Jesus and Mary....

St John Leonardi

All for God, all for the greater glory of God!

My God, be blessed, praised, adored, loved, served, and glorified forever! My God, I believe in you; I hope in you; I adore you; and I love you with all my heart! My God, I give myself completely to you, and I want to live for you alone.

Bd John Martin Moye

Providence of my God, admirable and divine Providence, Providence infinitely enlightened, foreseeing and providing for all, Providence infinitely wise, governing all with order, weight, and measure, I adore you in all your designs. I abandon myself to you without reserve. I place my destiny in your hands.

I confide to you the care of my body and my soul, my health and my reputation, my goods and my fortune, my life, my death, and especially my eternal salvation, firmly convinced that it cannot be better placed than in your hands.

I no longer desire to govern myself but to be governed in all things by your providence. I will not give myself up to useless anxiety or unnecessary cares, but doing for my part what you command, I confide to you the success of all my undertakings. I will await all from your goodness and lean entirely on your providence. I will not undertake anything that I have not confided to your care, and in all difficulties and doubts I will have recourse to you as a never-failing source of help.

I will place all my confidence in your providence, knowing that you will either preserve me from the evils I dread or give me the strength to bear them patiently and so make them salutary to me, turning them to my good and your glory. Moreover, I will fear only one evil—sin. I will always keep in mind this truth: all that happens to me is a disposition and an effect of your providence, firmly convinced that you take as much care of me as if I were the only one in the world.

And so, peaceful and contented in all, I will live and die under the reign and the direction of your divine providence. I will never again withdraw myself from it for a single instant. I will not anticipate it, nor forestall it, but wait patiently for the moment you have regulated and determined. I will allow your providence to govern my life without worry or overeagerness. All my attention will be to study and to follow your providence even in the least things.

Bd John Martin Moye

Be enlightened, new Jerusalem! Be enlightened, for the glory of the Lord has risen in you! Zion: leap, rejoice! And exult, all-holy *Theotokos*, for your child has risen again! O blessed, holy, and sweetest promise!—that you will be with us all the days of earth until the end!

These are your words, Christ, who cannot deceive, and trusting in them, with firm hope, we rejoice.

St John of Damascus

O wonder! The lamps of the divine attributes, though one in substance, are still distinct, each burning as the other, one being substantially the other. O abyss of delights, and the more abundant, the more their riches are gathered together in infinite simplicity and unity. There each one is so recognized and felt as not to hinder the feeling and recognition of the other; yea, rather everything in you is light that does not impede anything; and by reason of your pureness, O divine Wisdom, many things are known in you in one, for you are the treasury of the everlasting Father, 'the brightness of eternal light, the unspotted mirror of God's majesty, and the image of his goodness,' 'in the splendours.'

St John of the Cross

I

O Living Flame of Love,
That wounds tenderly
My soul in its inmost depth!
As you are no longer grievous,
Perfect your work, if it be your will,
Break the web of this sweet encounter.

II

O sweet burn!
O delicious wound!
O tender hand! O gentle touch!
Savouring of everlasting life,
And paying the whole debt,
By slaying you have changed death into life.

III

O lamps of fire,
In the splendours of which
The deep caverns of sense,
Dim and dark,
With unwonted brightness
Give light and warmth together to their Beloved!

IV

How gently and how lovingly
You wake in my bosom,
Where alone you secretly dwell;
And in your sweet breathing
Full of grace and glory,
How tenderly you fill me with your love.

St John of the Cross

I

My God, my Lord, do you remember
That I by faith have gazed upon your face—
Lacking which sight no bliss exists for me!

II

For since I saw you, live I in such sort
That there is naught can bring
Joy to my soul but for an hour, or moment!

III

God of my life! nothing can make me glad,
For all my gladness springs from sight of you,
And fails me because I have you not.

IV

If 'tis your will, my God, I live forlorn,
I'll take my longings even for my comfort
While dwelling in this world.

V

With me no happiness in aught shall bide
Except the hope of seeing you, my God,
Where I shall never dread to lose you more.

VI

When shall there dawn that most delicious day
When, O my Glory, I may joy in you,
Delivered from this body's heavy load?

VII

There will my bliss be measureless, entire,
At witnessing how glorious you are,
Wherein will lie the rapture of my life.

VIII

What will it be when I shall dwell with you,
Since suffering brings such happiness?
Upraise me, now, O Lord, into your heaven!

IX

Yet if my life can bring increase of glory
To your eternal Being,
In truth I do not wish that it should end.

X

The unending moment of the bliss of heaven
Will end my pain and anguish
So that I shall remember them no more.

XI

I went astray because I served you not,
As I have gained by knowing you, my God!
Henceforth I crave to love you ever more!

St John of the Cross

All that is bitter and painful I keep for your sake, and all that
is sweet and pleasant I keep for you.

St John of the Cross

'Let us so act, that, by the practice of this love, we may come
to see ourselves in your beauty in everlasting life.' That is: 'Let
me be so transformed in your beauty, that, being alike in
beauty, we may see ourselves both in your beauty; having your
beauty, so that, one beholding the other, each may see his own
beauty in the other, the beauty of both being yours only, and
mine absorbed in it. And thus I shall see you in your beauty,
and myself in your beauty, and you shall see me in your
beauty; and I shall see myself in you in your beauty, and you
yourself in me in your beauty; so shall I seem to be yourself in
your beauty, and you myself in your beauty; my beauty shall
be yours, yours shall be mine, and I shall be you in it, and you
myself in your own beauty; for your beauty will be my beauty,
and so we shall see, each the other, in your beauty.'

St John of the Cross

What ill or evil, Lord, can harm
This joyous heart that you alone can charm?
I love you more with every breath,
So how can I fear life or death?
To love you, Father, is to live and sing
The songs the angels sing their King.
God alone in every cell of me!
God alone! For all eternity!

St Louis Marie Grignion de Montfort

My God, I firmly believe that you are here present; I adore
you, and acknowledge you as my sovereign Lord and Master.
Amen.

St Louis Marie Grignion de Montfort

We offer you our simple praise, Lord Jesus,
for, unworthy as we are,
You have defended us from the errors of the pagans,
and in your mercy,
You have allowed us to come to this time of suffering
for the honour of your name.
As you have permitted us to share in the glory
of your saints,
We offer you glory and praise
and we commend to your keeping our lives and our souls.

St Lucian of Antioch

It is you alone, Lord, who has done it all.

St Madeleine Sophie Barat

May God's holy name be blessed!

St Marguerite d'Youville

I take you, O dearest Jesus, as my spouse for time and eternity.
I desire to approach you trustingly, as a bride her bridegroom,
to look to you in everything,
to listen to your holy voice in times of doubt,
to follow you willingly,
to remain in peace under your protection in all adversity, and
to seek only you in time and eternity. Amen.

Bd Maria Helena Stollenwerk

Blessed be God in everything!

St Maria Soledad Torres Acosta

Let us praise God, let us bless him in everything.

St Maria Soledad Torres Acosta

I invited the whole earth, to bless you, to serve you.
Forever and always, never to end!
With your love my heart made one.
I invited the entire sea, to bless you, to serve you.
Forever and always, never to end!
I called them, invited them, little birds of the air,
to bless you, to serve you.
Forever and always, never to end!
I called, I invited the star of the morn.
Forever and always, never to end!

…I called him, invited ungrateful man, to bless you,
to serve you, to praise and to love you,
Forever and always, never to end.

Bd Mariam Baouardy

My enraptured spirit contemplates all your works.
Who can speak of you, O God so great!
Omnipotent One, my soul is carried away!
His wonderful beauty delights my soul.
Who can tell what the Almighty looks upon?
One look!
You who gaze at me, come to me, a little nothing.
I cannot remain here on earth, my soul longing.
Call me close to you, awaken me.
You alone, my God, my all.
The heavens, the earth, the sun rejoice at your name so great.

I see you, supreme goodness: your gaze is maternal.
My Father, my Mother, it is in you that I sleep,
It is in you that I breathe. Awaken!
My soul is mad with yearning, it can do no more, take it.
When will we see him forever world without end!

Bd Mariam Baouardy

O great abyss, how captivating are your charms! May you be
blessed, O my great abyss, O abyss of goodness.

Bd Marie of the Incarnation

Blessed be the hour in which my Lord Jesus Christ took
human flesh, was born, died, and rose again, ascended into
heaven, and in which he instituted the most holy sacrament of
the Eucharist.

Bd Mary Ann of Jesus de Paredes y Flores, the Lily of Quito

Who would dare to imagine that you, O infinite, eternal God,
have loved me for centuries, or to be more precise, from
before the beginning of the centuries?

In fact, you have loved me ever since you have existed as
God; thus, you have always loved me and you shall always
love me!...

Your love for me was already there, even when I had no
existence, and precisely because you loved me, O good God,
you called me from nothingness to existence!...

For me you have created the skies scattered with stars, for
me the earth, the seas, the mountains, the streams, and all the
beautiful things on earth....

Still, this did not satisfy you: to show me close up that you loved me so tenderly, you came down from the purest delights of heaven to this tarnished and tearful world, you lived amidst poverty, hard work, and suffering; and finally, despised and mocked, you let yourself be suspended in torment on a vile scaffold between two criminals....

O God of love, you have redeemed me in this terrible, though generous, fashion!....

Who would venture to imagine it?

St Maximilian Kolbe

O Jesus, most glorious in your magnificence: I praise and bless your incomprehensible omnipotence, weak and helpless for us in the Passion. I adore and glorify your unsearchable wisdom, accounted foolishness for us. I praise and magnify your unutterable love, which submitted to hatred of all people for the sake of your elect. I praise and extol your meek and gentle mercy, sentenced to so fearful a death for humanity. I praise and I adore your ravishing sweetness, embittered for us by your most bitter death. Amen.

St Mechtilde

I long for you, O Lord God of my fathers, and Lord of mercy, who has deigned of your own glory and goodness, which provides for all, of your gracious condescension, with which you incline toward us, as a mediator bringing peace, to establish harmony between earth and heaven. I seek you, the great Author of all. With longing I expect you, who, with your word, embrace all things. I wait for you, the Lord of life and death. For you I search, the giver of the law, and the successor of the law. I hunger for you, who quickens the dead; I thirst for you, who refreshes the weary; I desire you, the Creator and Redeemer of mankind.

You are our God, and you we adore. You are our holy temple: in you we pray. You are our lawgiver: you we obey. You are God of all things the first. To know you is perfect righteousness: to know your power is the root of immortality. You are the One who, for our salvation, was made the headstone of the corner, precious and honourable, prophesied to Zion. All things are placed under you as their cause and author, as he who brought all things into being out of nothing, and gave to what was unstable a firm coherence; as the connecting band and preserver of that which has been brought into being; as the framer of things by nature different; as he who, with wise and steady hand, holds the helm of the uniters; as the very principle of all good order; as the unbreakable bond of concord and peace. For in you we live and move and have our being.

Wherefore, O Lord, my God, I will glorify you; I will praise your name, for you have done wonderful things. Your counsels of old are faithfulness and truth. You are clothed with majesty and honour. For what is more splendid for a king than a purple robe embroidered around with flowers, and a shining diadem? Or what for, God, who delights in mankind, is this merciful assumption of the manhood, illuminating with its resplendent rays those who sit in darkness and the shadow of death? Fitly did that temporal king and your servant once sing of you as the king eternal, saying, 'You are fairer than the children of humans,' who among people are very God and very Man. For you have girt, by your incarnation, your loins with righteousness, and anointed your veins with faithfulness, who yourself are very righteousness and truth, the joy and exultation of all.

Therefore, rejoice with me this day, O heavens, for the Lord has shown mercy to his people. Yea! let the clouds drop the dew of righteousness upon the world: let the foundations of the earth sound a trumpet blast in Hades, for the resurrection of those for whom sleep is come. Let the earth also cause compassion to spring up to its inhabitants; for I am filled with comfort; I am exceedingly joyful since I have seen you, the Saviour of mankind.

St Methodius

I desire to love you, my Lord, my light, my strength, my deliverer, my God, and my all.

What have I in heaven, O God, and what do I want besides you on earth?

My spirit and my body languish with yearning for your majesty.

You are the God of my heart, you are my portion, my inheritance for eternity. Amen.

St Paschal Baylon

You, Lord, have ever done all things well and will continue to do all things well for all eternity. My whole soul trusts you in life as in death.

Bd Pauline von Mallinckrodt

Lord, you know that you alone are the life of my soul, my highest love, my light, my God, my all! Without you life is so dead, so empty—without you, Lord, life is not worth living.

Bd Pauline von Mallinckrodt

O God...may you be praised for every struggle, for every suffering, as well as for every joy you send us, because both pain and joy come from your Father's heart. Both are for our salvation.

Bd Pauline von Mallinckrodt

To God the Father be glory through endless ages; eternal Son, may we sing your glorious praises; heavenly Spirit, to you be honour and glory. May the Holy Trinity be praised unceasingly through all eternity. Amen.

St Paulinus of Aquileia

Grant me grace, O Lord, to love you, my one hope, according to your command, with all my heart, all my soul, and all my strength. You are all my glory, my refuge, and my consolation, my best of friends, my soul's betrothed, all radiant and alluring, sweeter than honey. Delight of my heart, my soul's life and joy: you are my everlasting happiness and my soul's paradise, my loving creator, and all that I can desire.

St Peter of Alcantara

Father of your beloved and blessed Son, Jesus Christ, through whom we have received the knowledge of you, the God of angels and of powers and of the whole creation and the entire race of the righteous who live in your presence:

I bless you, that you have deemed me worthy of this day and hour, that I might receive a portion in the number of the martyrs, in the cup of Christ, unto the resurrection of eternal life both of body and of soul in the immortality of the Holy Spirit. Among these may I be received before you this day, in an acceptable, a rich sacrifice, as you, the faithful and true God, beforehand have prepared, and have revealed, and have fulfilled.

Wherefore, I praise you for everything: I bless you, I glorify you, through the eternal high priest, Jesus Christ, your beloved Son, and with him, in the Holy Spirit, be unto you your glory given: both now and for ages to come. Amen.

St Polycarp

See, the golden dawn is glowing
While the paly shades are going,
Which have led us far and long,
In a labyrinth of wrong.

May it bring us peace serene;
May it cleanse, as it is clean;
Plain and clear our words be spoke,
And our thoughts without a cloak.

So the day's account shall stand,
Guileless tongue and holy land,
Steadfast eyes and unbeguiled,
Flesh as of a little child.

There is One who from above
Watches how the still hours move
Of our day of service done,
From the dawn to setting sun.

To the Father, and the Son,
And the Spirit, Three and One,
As of old, and as in heaven,
Now and here be glory given!

St Prudentius
(The arrangement is Cardinal Newman's.)

God, you are with me and you can help me; you were with me
when I was taken, and you are with me now. You strengthen me.
    The God I serve is everywhere—in heaven and earth and
the sea, but he is above them all, for all live in him: all were
created by him, and by him only do they remain.
    I will worship only the true God; you will I carry in my
heart; no one on earth shall be able to separate me from you.

St Quirinus

O how merciful a Father thou art, to least orphans, how easy a
judge to repentant sinners, and how faithful a friend to sincere
lovers! It is undoubtedly true, that thou never leavest alone
that love thee, and thou lovest such as rest their love in thee.
They shall find thee liberal above desert, and bountiful beyond
hope: a measurer of thy gifts, not by their merits, but thy own
mercy.

St Robert Southwell

My tongue, O Lord, talketh of thee, because I have no other means to satisfy my desire, but to keep and observe the respect that is due unto thy glory. My understanding humbleth itself, and casting her eyes downwards, saith that it is not able to endure so great brightness, and that if it think and talk of thee, it is not with intent to comprehend what thou art, but to inflame the will the more in thy flame, the heat whereof is now somewhat felt, and the clear light whereof shall be seen in thy Kingdom, enjoying thee amongst those angelical hierarchies, and multitude of thy elect, in that eternal bliss and celestial Jerusalem, which is thy glory, where thou livest and reignest for evermore. Amen.

St Robert Southwell

Oh, how lovely are thy habitations, my God and Lord of virtues, my soul fainteth for desire to enter into thy house. Thy sight will recollect all my thoughts, and gather together my whole strength, that I may entirely employ myself upon. For this shall be no small part of blessedness, to see that the least hair of my head shall not perish, nor that there shall be nothing in me unrewarded.

St Robert Southwell

You, O Christ, are the kingdom of heaven; you the land promised to the gentle; you the grazing-lands of paradise; you the hall of the celestial banquet; you the ineffable marriage-chamber; you the table set for all; you the bread of life; you the unheard-of drink; you both the urn for the water and the life-giving water; you, moreover, the inextinguishable lamp for each of the saints; you the garment and the crown and the one

who distributes the crowns; you the joy and the rest; you the
delight and the glory; you the gaiety and the mirth; and your
grace, grace of the Spirit of all sanctity, will shine in their
midst, and all will shine brightly to the degree of their faith,
their asceticism, their hope and their love, their purification
and their illumination by your Spirit.

St Symeon the New Theologian

My God, my blessedness: I have realized that whoever
undertakes anything for the sake of earthly things, or to earn
the praise of others, is self-deceived. Today, one thing pleases
the world; tomorrow, it is another: what is on one occasion
praised is denounced upon another.

Blessed are you, my Lord, my God, for you are
unchangeable in all eternity!

Whoever faithfully serves you until the end shall enjoy life
without end in all eternity.

St Teresa of Ávila

The cross is my sure salvation. The cross I ever adore. The
cross of my Lord is with me. The cross is my refuge.

St Thomas Aquinas

Into your hands, O Lord, I commend my spirit.

For the name of Jesus, and in defence of the Church, I am
willing to die.

St Thomas Becket

PRAYERS
OF
SORROW

Alas, O my Lord, how true it is that we are in darkness, and I have not performed any work without offending you: what then remains for me to do? O my God, though I have offended you so much in this day, yet I will not commit this last and greatest offence, which would be if I should not confide in you, and in your mercy. I know well, O Lord, that I deserve no pardon, but the blood that you shed for me will make me hope in you, and that you will forgive me.

St Mary Magdalene dei Pazzi

Behold the wounds of my soul, O Lord. Your eye sees everything, and alive and full of energy it reaches the very division between the soul and spirit. Surely you see in my soul, O Lord, the traces of past sins, the perils of present ones, and the sources and causes of future ones. You see these things, O Lord, and thus I wish you to see them, for you, the searcher of all hearts, know that I would hide nothing from your eyes even if I could avoid their gaze. Woe to those who wish to be hidden from the Lord, for they do not succeed in not being seen by you but rather in not being punished and healed by you. Behold me, O sweet Lord, behold me! For I hope that in your loving-kindness, O most merciful one, you will behold me either as a loving physician to heal, a kind teacher to correct, or an indulgent father to pardon.

This is why, O fountain of piety, confident in your sweet powerful mercy and most merciful power, I ask in virtue of your sweet name and of the mystery of your sacred humanity that, mindful of your kindness and unmindful of my ingratitude, you forgive me my sins and heal the languors of my soul. And may your sweet grace bring strength and fortitude to me against the vices and evil passions that still war against my soul because of my old evil habits and daily negligence, because of the weakness of my nature or the secret malice of the devil. Let me not consent to them. Let them not reign in my mortal body. I must not make my bodily powers over to sin, to be the instruments of harm, until you perfectly cure my infirmities, heal my wounds, repair my deformities.

May your good and sweet Spirit descend into my heart and prepare there a habitation for himself, clean from every defilement of flesh and of spirit and pour into it an increase of

faith, hope, and charity, compunction, piety, and love of
humanity. May he extinguish the heat of concupiscence by the
dew of his benediction. May he kill the commotions of lust
and carnal affections by his power. May he bestow fervour and
discretion upon me in labours, watchings, and fastings;
devotion and efficacy in loving and praising you, in praying,
meditating, and directing every thought and action to you.
May he grant me perseverance in all these things to the end of
my life.

St Aelred of Rievaulx

O adorable heart of my Saviour! How it displeases me to have
offended you by my many sins. How it saddens me to have
outraged you with foolish talk! I deserve to be abandoned. But
you did not abandon me, and for this I give you glory. My lips
will always resound your praise since I have been saved by
your most precious blood.

Bd Aloysius Guanella

Eternal God, I offer you my whole heart. But what a sorry
heart I have to offer! A heart created to love you, but, far from
loving you, so often rebellious toward you! But look, my Jesus!
If my poor heart was once rebellious, now it is full of grief and
repentance for the displeasure it has given you, and I am
firmly resolved to obey you and love you. Draw me to your
love! Do it, I beg you, through the love you bore me while
dying on the cross for me.

I love you, my Jesus; I love you with all my heart.

St Alphonsus de' Liguori

O my beloved Jesus, O God, who has loved me with love exceeding! What more can you do to make yourself loved by ungrateful people? If we loved you, all the churches would be continually filled with people prostrate on the ground adoring and thanking you, burning with love for you, and seeing you with the eyes of faith, hidden in a tabernacle. But no, we are forgetful of you and your love. We are ready enough to try to win the favour of a person from whom we hope for some miserable advantage, while we leave you, Lord, abandoned and alone. If only by my devotion I could make reparation for such ingratitude! I am sorry that I also have been careless and ungrateful. In the future I will change my ways, I will devote myself to your service as much as possible. Inflame me with your holy love, so that from this day forward I may live only to love and to please you. You deserve the love of all hearts. If at one time I have despised you, I now desire nothing but to love you. O my Jesus, you are my love and my only good, 'my God and my all.'

St Alphonsus de' Liguori

O my beloved God, you are beauty itself, goodness itself, and love itself. How can I love anything but you! How foolish I have been. In my past I have offered numberless insults to you; and I now promise and desire to repeat every moment of my life that I desire you only, O my God, and nothing more.

St Alphonsus de' Liguori

O Jesus, my redeemer, you have suffered so much pain, such great ignominy for my sake! And I have loved the pleasures and the goods of this earth to such a degree that, to have them, I have often forgotten you and trampled upon your grace.

But since you continued to pursue me, even after I despised you, I cannot fear that you will reject me now that I seek you and wish to love you with all my heart and am sorry for having offended you.

I accept, now, all the pains and sufferings that may come into my life. Let me suffer with you in this life that in the next I may rejoice with you and love you for all eternity.

St Alphonsus de' Liguori

My dear and beloved Jesus, my treasure, because of my offences against you, I don't deserve to be allowed to love you any more. But thanks to your merits, I beg you, make me worthy of your pure love. I love you above all things; and I repent with my whole heart of having once despised you and driven you from my soul; but now I love you more than myself; I love you with all my heart, O infinite good! I love you, I love you, I love you, and I desire nothing more than to love you perfectly; nor do I fear anything except seeing myself deprived of your holy love.

O my most loving redeemer, make me know how great and good you are, and how great is the love you have borne me so as to make me love you.

Ah, my God, don't let me live any longer ungrateful to you for all your goodness! I have offended you enough, I don't ever want to leave you again; I wish to spend all the remaining years

of my life loving you and pleasing you. My Jesus, my love, help
me; help a sinner who wishes to love you and to be all yours.

St Alphonsus de' Liguori

To you, O Lord, I show my wounds. I know my many and
great sins for which I am afraid. My trust is in your mercies, of
which there is no end. Look, therefore, on me with eyes of
your mercy, O Lord, Jesus Christ, God and man. Hear me,
whose trust is in you: upon me, mercy!—who am full of
misery and sin.

St Ambrose

O Lord, who has mercy upon all, take away from me my sins,
and mercifully kindle in me the fire of your Holy Spirit.
    Take away from me the heart of stone: give me a heart of
flesh, a heart to love, to adore you, Lord, a heart to delight in
you, to follow, to rejoice in you, for the sake of Jesus Christ.
Amen.

St Ambrose

Lord Jesus Christ, who stretched out your hands on the cross
and redeemed us by your blood: Forgive me, a sinner, for
none of my thoughts are hidden from you. Pardon I ask,
pardon I hope for, pardon I trust to have. You who are full of
pity and mercy: spare me, and forgive.

St Ambrose

O Father, most merciful, who, in the beginning, created us; who, by the passion of your only-begotten Son, created us anew: Work in us now, we beseech you, both to will and to do your good pleasure! And because we are weak, and can do no good thing on our own, grant us your grace. Grant us your heavenly benediction, that in whatever work we undertake we may do all to your honour and your glory; that, being kept from sin, daily increasing in good works, so long as we live in the body, we may always give service to you—and after our departure we may receive pardon for all our sins, attaining life eternal: through him who, with you and the Holy Spirit, lives and reigns, God, for evermore. Amen.

St Anselm of Canterbury

O Lord Jesus Christ, our redemption, our salvation: We praise you and we give you thanks! And though we be unworthy of your great gifts, and though we cannot offer you your due devotion, yet let your loving-kindness fill that which our weakness attempts. Before you, O Lord our God, all our desire is disclosed, and whatever our heart wills rightly, it is of your gift. Grant that we may love you as you command us. Let not your gift be unfruitful in us, Lord! Perfect what you have begun! Give us what you have made us to long after! Convert our tepidity to fervent love of you: for the glory of your holy name. Amen.

St Anselm of Canterbury

O merciful, almighty Father, you pour down your benefits upon us; forgive the unthankfulness with which we have requited your goodness.

We have remained before you with dead, unfeeling hearts, not kindled with the love of your gentle and enduring goodness. Turn to us, O merciful Father.

Make us hunger and thirst for you with our whole hearts. With all our longings let us desire you. Make us serve you— you alone—with all of our heart. With all our zeal help us desire only those things that are pleasing to you.

We ask this for the sake of your only-begotten Son, to whom, with you and the Holy Spirit, be all honour and all glory, Lord, for evermore. Amen.

St Anselm of Canterbury

Come then, Lord, sustain your people, bought with the price of your own blood.

Save your people, Lord, and bless your inheritance: govern them and lift them up unto eternity.

Deign, O Lord, to keep us from sin this day.

Have mercy on us, Lord, have mercy on us.

Let your mercy come upon us, Lord, as we have hoped in you.

In you, O Lord, I have trusted; I shall never be put to shame.

St Anthony Mary Claret

O Holy Spirit, love of God: Infuse your grace!

O, plentifully descend into my heart! Enlighten the dark corners of this neglected dwelling. Dwell in that soul that longs to be your temple! Water that barren soil, overrun with weeds and briars and lost to fruitfulness for want of cultivating. Make it fruitful with your gracious beams, your dew from heaven. O come, refreshment of those who languish and faint! Come, star and guide of those that sail in the tempestuous sea, the world; You, only haven of the tossed and the shipwrecked!

Come, Holy Spirit, in much mercy! Make me fit to receive you. Amen.

St Augustine

Be mindful, O Lord, of my unworthy self, according to the abundance of your mercies. Forgive all my offences, deliberate or accidental, and withdraw not the grace of your Holy Spirit because of my sins.

St Basil the Great

O Lord, I place myself in your hands and dedicate myself to you. I pledge myself to do your will in all things—to love the Lord God with all my heart, all my soul, all my strength.

Not to kill or steal; not to covet or bear false witness. To honour all persons. Not to do to another what I would not wish done to myself. To chastise the body and not to seek after pleasures.

To love fasting and to relieve the poor; to clothe the naked and to visit the sick; to bury the dead and to help those in trouble. To console the sorrowing and to hold myself aloof from worldly ways. To prefer nothing to the love of Christ.

Not to give way to anger nor to foster a desire for revenge; not to entertain deceit in the heart nor to make a false peace; not to forsake charity nor to swear, lest I swear falsely.

To speak the truth with heart and tongue and not to return evil for evil; to do no evil and, indeed, even to bear patiently any injury done to me. To love my enemies and not to curse those who curse me—but rather to bless them.

To bear persecution for justice's sake and not to be proud. Not to delight in intoxicating drink, nor to be an overeater; not to be lazy or slothful; not to be a murmurer or a detractor.

To put my trust in God and to refer the good I see in myself to God; to refer any evil in myself to myself, and to fear the day of judgment. To be in dread of hell and to desire eternal life with ardent longing; to keep death before my eyes daily and to keep constant watch over my words and deeds.

To remember that God sees me everywhere and so to call upon Christ for defence against evil thoughts that spring up in my heart. To guard my tongue against wicked speech and, indeed, to avoid much speaking. To avoid idle talk and not try to be considered clever.

To read only what is good to read and to look at only what is good to see. To pray often. To ask forgiveness daily for my sins and to look for ways to amend my life. To obey my superiors in all legitimate things, not to be thought holy so much as to be holy.

To fulfil the commandments of God through good works. To love chastity and to hate no one. Not to be jealous or envious of anyone, nor to love strife and pride. To honour the aged and to pray for my enemies. To make peace after a quarrel before sunset and never to despair of your mercy, O God of mercy. Amen.

St Benedict

Eternal Father, by the blood of Jesus have mercy; sign us with the blood of the immaculate lamb Jesus Christ, as you signed the people of Israel, to deliver them from death....

Eternal Father, by the blood of Jesus have mercy; save us from the shipwreck of the world, as you saved Noah from the universal deluge....

Eternal Father, by the blood of Jesus have mercy; deliver us from the plagues that we have deserved for our sins, as you delivered Lot from the flames of Sodom....

Eternal Father, by the blood of Jesus have mercy; comfort us under our present necessities and troubles, as you comforted Job, Anna, and Tobias in their afflictions....

Eternal Father, by the blood of Jesus, have mercy; you who would not will the death of a sinner, but rather that he should be converted and live, grant us through your mercy time for penance; that, filled with contrition and penance for our sins, which are the cause of all our evils, we may live in the holy faith, hope, charity, and peace of our Lord Jesus Christ....

Precious blood of Jesus, our love, cry unto the Divine Father for mercy, pardon, grace, and peace for us, for N., and for all the world....

Eternal Father, I offer you the blood of Jesus Christ in discharge of all my debt of sin, for the wants of Holy Church, and for the conversion of sinners. Glory to the Father, to the Son, and to the Holy Spirit, as it was in the beginning, is now, and ever shall be, world without end. Amen.

St Benedict Joseph Labre

My God! when I pause and reflect upon my numberless
shortcomings and your justice, I am appalled; fear paralyses
me. My God! have mercy upon my misery and frailty. Let
suffering and trial be my lot. They alone can destroy the 'old
man' in me. Divine life is only possible in making the sacrifice
of human nature. There is no alternative; I must make this
sacrifice if I desire to save my soul.

St Bernadette Soubirous of Lourdes

Help us, O Lord our God, since we cannot flee from the body,
nor the body flee from us: we must carry it about, because it is
bound up with us. We cannot destroy it; we are forced to
preserve it. But the world surrounds us, and assails us through
the five gateways of sense. Alas! everywhere we are in conflict,
everywhere darts fly against us, everywhere there are
temptations, there are snares! Deliver us, we beseech you,
from our enemies; defend us from all dangers to the soul and
to the body, Lord, that at length we may come to your eternal
rest, through Jesus Christ, our Lord. Amen.

St Bernard of Clairvaux

O holy Lord, almighty Father, eternal God! through your
liberality and that of your Son, who for me endured suffering
and death, through the surpassing holiness of his mother, and
through the merits of blessed Francis, and of all the saints,
grant me, a sinner, undeserving of all your benefits, that I may
love you alone, and always thirst for your love; that I may
constantly feel in my heart the benefit of your passion; that I
may acknowledge my misery, and desire to be trampled upon

and despised by all men; that nothing but sin may sadden my
heart. Amen.

St Bonaventure

O Jesus, fountain of wisdom, source of knowledge, giver of
good counsel: Let me hear from now on your voice
resounding always in my ear!

I consider how I was led astray by the accursed call of those
who said and sang, 'Come! let us rejoice in the good that is
still existent! We will crown ourselves with roses, before they
wither, and the bloom of time shall not escape us.' I heard
their voice, and did not understand that it was all vain and
foolish, for those joys passed swiftly and like a shadow
vanished. And what did they profit those who enjoyed them?
What fruit had these from the things of which they are now
ashamed?

O Lord God, light of my heart, bread of my soul, strength
of my spirit: I did not love you; I fled from you and went after
strange loves. And as I chased after strange love, I heard the
mocking call: 'Right, right. the friendship of this world is a
frivolous intrigue in your sight!'

O! what is more wretched than the one who is not
concerned about their own wretchedness!

Yet despite all this, you, O most lovable Lord, have not
forsaken me! Now, like Augustine, I beseech you: Grant that
through love I may inwardly feel what I outwardly perceive
through the intellect, and that I may experience with my will
what I realize with my understanding!

St Bonaventure

O Jesus! loveliest of all beauty: Wash me more and more from my iniquity! Cleanse me of my sin, that, purified by you, I may approach you, the pure one, and thus may be made worthy to dwell in your heart all the days of my life, that I may both see and do your will. Amen.

St Bonaventure

My Love, I can bear anything else, but to have offended you is too horrible and unbearable. Give me any other penance, but not that of seeing I have offended you. I do not wish to have committed the offences I have committed against you. I cannot consent to have ever offended you. At the hour of death show me rather the devils with all their terrors and torments. I consider them as nothing in comparison with the sight of the least offence against you.

St Catherine of Genoa

Have mercy on me, Lord, for I have sinned.

St Catherine of Siena

O ineffable Deity! I am all sin, and unworthy to address you, but you can make me worthy. O Lord, punish my sins, and regard not my miseries. I have one body, and to you I give it: behold my blood, behold my flesh; destroy it, annihilate it, separate it bone from bone for the sake of those for whom I pray.

St Catherine of Siena

I. *To the Wound in the Right Hand*
Praise be to you, O Jesus Christ, for the most sacred wound in your right hand. By this adorable wound, and by your most sacred passion, pardon me all the sins I have committed against you in thought, word, and deed, and all negligence in your service, and all sensuality for which I have been to blame whether asleep or awake. Grant that I may be able to recall with devotion your most pitiful death and sacred wounds; grant me the grace to mortify my body, and so to offer a pledge of my gratitude to you, who lives and reigns world without end. Amen. *Our Father* and *Hail Mary.*

II. *To the Wound in the Left Hand*
Praise and glory be to you, O sweetest Jesus Christ, for the most sacred wound in your left hand. By this adorable wound, have mercy on me, and deign to root out of my heart everything displeasing to you. Give me the victory over your perverse enemies, so that with your grace I may be able to overcome them; and by the merits of your most pitiful death save me from all the dangers of my present and future life; and then, grant that I may share your glory in heaven, who lives and reigns for ever and ever. Amen. *Our Father* and *Hail Mary.*

III. *To the Wound in the Right Foot*
Praise and glory be to you, O sweet Jesus Christ, for the most sacred wound in your right foot; and by that adorable wound, grant me grace to do penance for my sins. And by your most pitiful death I devoutly beg of you to keep me, your poor servant, united, night and day, to your holy will, and to remove afar off every misfortune of body and soul. And when the day of wrath shall come, receive me into your mercy, and

lead me to eternal happiness. Who lives and reigns world without end. Amen. *Our Father* and *Hail Mary*.

IV. *To the Wound in the Left Foot*
Praise and glory be to you, most merciful Jesus Christ, for the most sacred wound in your left foot; and by this adorable wound, grant me the grace of a full pardon, that with your aid I may deserve to escape the sentence of eternal reprobation. I pray you, moreover, by your most holy death, O my loving redeemer, that I may be able before my death to receive the sacrament of your body and blood, after confession of my sins, and with perfect repentance and purity of body and mind. Grant that I may merit also to receive the holy anointing, for my eternal salvation, O Lord, who lives and reigns world without end. Amen. *Our Father* and *Hail Mary*.

V. *To the Wound in the Sacred Side*
Praise and glory be to you, most loving Jesus Christ, for the most sacred wound in your side, and by that adorable wound, and by your infinite mercy, which you made known in the opening of your breast to the soldier Longinus, and so to us all, I pray you, O most gentle Jesus, that having redeemed me by baptism from original sin, so now by your precious blood, which is offered and received throughout the world, deliver me from all evils, past, present, and to come. And by your most bitter death give me a lively faith, a firm hope, and a perfect charity, so that I may love you with all my heart, and all my soul, and all my strength; make me firm and steadfast in good works, and grant me perseverance in your service, so that I may be able to please you always. Amen. *Our Father* and *Hail Mary*.
                                                        St Clare of Assisi

Give me, O my God, that tenderness of conscience which will dread even the shadow of sin; make in me, or help me to obtain that severity and uprightness of soul which will not allow nor forgive in itself any thing that offends you. It is true that I must deny myself, retrench many things agreeable to my inclinations, and refrain from many gratifications which seem even innocent.

In many circumstances, I must humble my spirit, suppress the sentiments of my heart, weigh my words, restrain my eyes and mortify my senses. But Lord, can I purchase too dear this double advantage of offending you less and preserving my soul? The happiness of pleasing you and the peace of my conscience will make amends for all and supply the peace of all.

St Elizabeth Ann Bayley Seton

Before my offences
Are brought against me
At the tribunal of justice;
And cause me to stand
In the presence of the judge
With confusion of face:—
    Have mercy on me, O Lord, for you are abundant in mercy!

Before you shall close
Your door against me,
You Son of God;
And I shall become
Food for the fire
That dies not in Hell:—
    Have mercy on me, O Lord, for you are abundant in mercy!

Before the wheel of time
Shall run its course
Above the well;
And the pitcher
Of all tribes of humanity
Be broken at the fountain:—
    Have mercy on me, O Lord, for you are abundant in mercy!

Before those who have made
A vain profession
Shall cry, 'Lord! Lord!'
And you answer them,
'I know not
Who you are':—
    Have mercy on me, O Lord, for you are abundant in mercy!

Before the mighty hosts
Shall go forth in the presence
Of the Son of the King;
And shall gather together
Our unhappy race
Before the judgment-seat:—
    Have mercy on me, O Lord, for you are abundant in mercy!

Before the dust
Shall return to the earth
And we become but clay;
And the forms of humankind
Now so beautiful
Are turned to corruption:—
    Have mercy on me, O Lord, for you are abundant in mercy!

Before the withering blast
Of death shall smite you
As if you were a tree;
And your body shall put forth
Diseases that presage
The season of death:—
　　Have mercy on me, O Lord, for you are abundant in mercy!

Before the brilliant sun
Shall become darkened
In the expanse on high;
Let your light appear,
And chase away the gloom
That obscures my intellect:—
　　Have mercy on me, O Lord, for you are abundant in mercy!

Before the voice of the trumpet
Shall shout aloud
To announce your coming;
O Lord Jesus,
Have pity on your servants
Who pray earnestly to you:—
　　Have mercy on me, O Lord, for you are abundant in mercy!
　　　　　　　　　　　　　　　　St Ephrem the Syrian

O Lord, we entreat of your goodness
That you will forgive our sins,
And pass by our follies.
Open to us, O Lord,
The door of your tender mercies,
That there may come to us

Seasons of refreshing.
And if indeed, O Lord,
You open the door to the penitent,
In your mercy receive our petition!

St Ephrem the Syrian

May my sins not be revealed
   to my brethren on that day,
—yet by this we show
   how contemptible we are, Lord;
if our sins are revealed to you,
   from whom can we hide them?
I have made shame
   an idol for myself;
grant me, Lord, to fear you,
   for you are mighty.
May I feel shame and self-reproach
   before you, for you are gentle.

St Ephrem the Syrian

O Lord: Be merciful to me, for henceforth I resolve to be more faithful to you. I will satisfy myself no longer with desires, but will put my resolutions into practice. I promise to relieve the poor, to do penance, and to sin no more. I will instruct the erring and will say to my own heart, and to the hearts of others: 'Can you treat your saviour more cruelly than birds of prey do the tender doves? Can you act so heartlessly to this Divine Dove, who nestles on the cross, as to tear his heart with the teeth of your impiety?' No, Lord: henceforth, I will comfort

and help your poor, by my deeds as truly as my words, and I
will strive, with all earnestness, to destroy and to overcome
sin, both in myself and in others.

St Francis de Sales

Ah, Lord: All that I hitherto have suffered has tended only to
my destruction, marred, as it has been, by sin. But now, dear
Lord, I return to you. You surely will yet save me! Your will
shall be done. I will follow out your designs and labour to
conform my will to yours. O most sweet will of my God: Be
you forever done! O, that I may do your will this day and
always in every perfection! O goodness most pleasing! be it as
you have willed. O eternal will! live and reign in every will of
mine and over every will of mine, now and forever.

St Francis de Sales

O incomprehensible love of my God, what can I do to love
you and you love me! I am not able to rise above my miserable
wretchedness before your adorable love. My well-beloved love,
you are so great that I do not even dare to think that I would
be able to do something for you. But you, most adorable love,
do with me and in me whatever you wish. Come, Lord Jesus,
and live in your poor servant.

Ven. Francis Libermann

O Jesus, my adorable Lord, I too am a miserable creature, despicable in the eyes of human beings and all your creatures. Like the woman at the well, I've come to draw water, heavenly water, at the well of my gentle saviour. Reveal yourself to me also and teach me what I need to know in order to do what is agreeable in your eyes and those of your heavenly Father.

Ven. Francis Libermann

Behold me at your feet, O Lord, begging for pity and mercy! What will you lose in granting me a great love for you, a profound humility, great purity of heart, mind and body; fraternal charity, intense sorrow for having offended you, and the grace to offend you no more?—What will you lose, O my God, by enabling me to receive worthily your Son in Holy Communion?—in assisting me to act through love of you in all my thoughts, works, penances, and prayers?—by granting me the grace of loving your holy mother most tenderly and trustfully; the grace of final perseverance in my vocation, and of dying a good and holy death?

I am a beggar asking for alms, covered with sores and rags. O see my misery! Here is my proud head, my cold heart, yes, my stony heart. Here is my mind filled with worldly thoughts, my will inclined only to evil, my body rebellious to every good work.

Help me, O my God!…do help me to correct myself. This grace I ask through your own goodness, through your infinite mercy. To obtain it, I offer you the merits of Jesus Christ, our saviour and Lord. I have no merits of my own, I am destitute; but his wounds will be my plea; 'Your wounds, O Lord, are my merits!' Had I shed my blood for love of you, like your

Son, would you not grant me this favour? How much more ought you to hear me now, since he shed his for me?

Are you not he who has promised in your gospel that whatsoever I ask for the good of my soul you will grant: 'Ask and you shall receive…'? Now, as you cannot withdraw your word, I beseech you to hear me. I beseech you through your infinite goodness; through the heart of your Son wounded with love for me; through the infinite charity of your eternal Spirit; through the love you bear your most holy daughter Mary; and for the honour of the whole heavenly court, into which I ask you one day to admit me. Amen.

St Gabriel Possenti

O Jesus, if I but considered attentively your immense solicitude for me, how greatly should I not excel in every virtue? Pardon me, O Jesus, so much carelessness, pardon such great ignorance. My God, Jesus my love, uncreated goodness, what would have become of me if you had not drawn me to yourself? Open your heart to me, open to me your sacramental breast; I open mine to you.

St Gemma Galgani

O Lord, enter not into judgment with your servant! But be merciful and forgive me! Look upon my contrite heart and forgive all my faults, all my trespasses, my every thoughtless word.

Correct my errors! Repair the scandals I may have given.

Bd George Matulaitis

Since I have so grievously insulted you, O most tender and loving God, by my manifold sins and negligences, I am ready now to make perfect satisfaction to your divine justice to the utmost of my ability. To this end I will faithfully and most reverently perform the penance appointed me by my confessor in your name; and I wish that I could perform it with so great devotion and love as to give you an honour and delight greater than the insult and outrage of my sins! And that this may be so, I unite and blend this my penance with all the works of satisfaction that your beloved Son accomplished during the three-and-thirty years of his life on earth, and in union with his fastings, his watchings, and his prayers, I offer you this, my penance and my prayer. Look down, therefore, O most loving Father, upon me, your most indebted debtor, now prostrate at your feet, desiring to make you adequate satisfaction and reparation for all the insults and injuries I have done you; and grant me strength and grace to say this prayer according to your most holy will. Amen.

St Gertrude of Helfta

Lord, I am not worthy to receive the least of your gifts; but I beseech you, by the merits and prayers of all here present, to pierce my heart with the arrow of your love.

St Gertrude of Helfta

I have distrusted your promises, O God of truth, as if you were a man who could lie, or fail in your fidelity!
Alas! I have also offended the goodness with which you have heard my unworthy prayers so favourably, by hardening

my heart against your will, and, as I ought to declare with tears in my eyes, sometimes pretending not to understand your will, lest the reproaches of my conscience should oblige me to obey it.

I have also despised the aid of your most glorious Mother, and that of the blessed spirits whom you have sent to me; and I have been so unhappy as to prove an obstacle even to my earthly friends, on whom I have leaned, instead of relying on you alone; and far from increasing my gratitude and my vigilance over my faults, on seeing that your charity continued your favours, notwithstanding my negligence, I, on the contrary, returned you evil for good, like a tyrant, or rather like a demon, and had the hardihood to live even more carelessly....

And now, O adorable creator of my soul, permit the groans of my heart to rise even to heaven in expiation of all these faults, and of others that you may yet bring to my recollection. Accept my grief for the immense number of offences that I have committed against the nobleness of your divine goodness. I offer it to you, with all the gratitude and all the reverence that you have enabled me, for all in heaven, on earth, and in the deep, through the merit of your beloved Son, and by the power of the Holy Spirit.

St Gertrude of Helfta

O most compassionate Jesus: Since in your unsearchable wisdom you know more clearly and more fully than I, or anyone, the extent of human frailty, I implore you to have manifold compassion on my manifold frailty, to supply all my defects and shortcomings. Offer to your most gracious Father,

O Jesus so filled with pity, the most becoming silence of your
holy lips, in expiation of all the sins I have committed, and in
supply of all the good I have omitted, by frivolous and vain
conversation. Offer, O good Jesus, the modesty of your most
holy ears for all the sins I have committed by hearing. Offer
also the reserve of your eyes for all the stains I have contracted
by wandering and forbidden looks. Offer the caution and
deliberation of your hands and feet, for all the sins that I have
committed in my daily actions or in my daily walk. Lastly, O
most loving Jesus, offer to his glorious Majesty your deified
heart, for all the sins that I have committed by thought, will,
or desire. Amen.

St Gertrude of Helfta

O God, who scourges our faults with strokes of love, to
cleanse us from our iniquities: Enable us to profit by these
strokes, and to rejoice in your consolation speedily!

St Gregory the Great

Look down, O sovereign creator of the world, our ruler, and
cast out from us all sinful sloth. We implore you, all-holy
Christ, to forgive our sins....

You see the evil we have done; we lay bare our secret faults;
sighing, we pour forth our prayers; pardon whatever we have
done amiss.

Grant this, O Father, only Son and Spirit, God of grace, to
whom all worship shall be offered in every time and place.
Amen.

St Gregory the Great

Remember, O Lord, my poverty: forgive me my sins. The place where iniquity abounds, let your grace abound. Do not take away from your people the grace of the Holy Spirit. Have mercy on us, O God our saviour; have mercy on us, O God our saviour; have mercy on us, O God our saviour: give to your people singleness of heart!

St Gregory Nazianzen

Ah, fathomless clemency, today I offer your innocent death to your heavenly Father in exchange for my guilty life. Lord, I address you with the thief: 'Remember, remember me in your kingdom. Reject me not because of my misdeeds, forgive me all my sins, and open for me your heavenly paradise.'

Bd Henry Suso

O my refuge, my protector, and my redeemer, be mindful of the infinite love that induced you to endure this most bitter death on the cross for my sake. Forgive all the sins that I, miserable sinner, have committed, and shelter me from future sins and evils in the wound of your side. Direct my path in this restless vale to a holy end, and permit me in eternity to enjoy the rapture of your beatific vision. Amen.

Bd Henry Suso

O delightful splendour of eternal light, for my sake you are now completely extinguished. Extinguish in me all sinful concupiscence.

O pure, sparkling mirror of the divine majesty, I have defiled you. Purify the serious defects of my crimes.

O lovely, luminous image of the Father's goodness, you are soiled and horribly disfigured. Repair the disfigured, faded image of my soul.

O innocent lamb, you are pitiably abused. Make amends for and redeem my guilty, sinful life.

O King of kings and Lord of lords, my soul beholds you living here, cold and miserable in death's rigidity. Grant me the favour that, as my soul now tearfully embraces you in your hour of darkness, so it may be joyfully embraced by you in your eternal brightness.

Bd Henry Suso

O Jesus, my dearest Love, my saving wisdom, word of the Father, beginning and end of all things, look upon me with the eyes of your mercy and see that I am a poor man, a speck of dust, a weak mortal. [Our] salvation rests not in [our] own strength but in your merciful forgiveness. Ah, Lord, remember the bitter death that you endured for me, a poor sinner, and give me the grace to persevere in the good that I have begun. O my mercy, do not forsake me. O my refuge, do not depart from me. O my redeemer, help me, give me the grace to die to the world and descend with you into the tomb. There I will be secure from all my enemies, and neither affliction nor distress will ever separate me from you. The strength of our love must conquer death. The bond of our love must remain firm between us for all eternity. Amen.

Bd Henry Suso

Pardon me, O perfections of my God, for having preferred imperfect and vile creatures to you!

Pardon me, O justice of my God, for having outraged you by my crimes!

Pardon me, O holiness of my God, pardon me for having so long stained your sight's purity by my sins!

Pardon me, O mercy of my God, for having despised so long your mercy's voice!

In deep sorrow and contrition, I cast myself at your feet: have mercy on me. Amen.

St Ignatius of Loyola

O Lord God! You are infinitely wise: I adore you, who have tolerated my ignorance.

O Lord God! You are infinitely just: I adore you, who have not chastised my iniquity.

O Lord God! You are infinitely powerful: I adore you, who have deigned to spare my weakness.

O Lord God! You are infinitely good: I adore you, who have pardoned me all my malice and my sins.

O Lord God: I thank you that the swords of your angels of justice have not slain me.

O Lord God: I thank you because the saints, your friends, have prayed and made intercession for me, who was your enemy.

O Lord God: I thank you that your heavens, your stars, your sun have not refused to shine on me. I thank you for having placed the whole of creation at my service: I have caused it to groan beneath the burden of my sin—and yet it has not risen up against me. I thank you that the very earth has not opened beneath my feet to precipitate me into the lowest depths of hell, where I indeed deserve to be eternally.

I behold before me, O my God, the mystery of the infinite depths of your mercy. I return thanks to you for having preserved my life until this day, for having granted me repentance for my sins.

O Lord God: How great has been, how incomprehensible remains your pity for me! Amen.

St Ignatius of Loyola

Father, in union with all those who celebrate the Eucharist, I wish to offer myself, a small victim, with Jesus, the victim:

- in atonement for error and scandal spread throughout the world through the misuse of the media of social communication;
- to appeal to your mercy for those persons who, deceived and seduced by the influence of these instruments, stray from your fatherly love;
- for the conversion of those persons who in the use of these instruments reject the teaching of Christ and his Church and thus warp the minds, the hearts, and the undertakings of men and women;
- that we may follow him alone whom you, Father, in your boundless love, sent into the world, saying, 'This is my beloved Son, hear him';
- to acknowledge and to make known that Jesus alone, the word incarnate, is the perfect teacher, the trustworthy way who leads to knowledge of you, Father, and to a partaking of your life;

- that there be in the Church an increase in the number of priests, religious, and laypersons who, consecrated as apostles of social communication, will make resound throughout the world the message of salvation;
- that all those who work within the framework of social communication may grow in holiness and wisdom and bear witness to an authentic Christian life;
- that well aware of our insufficiency and unworthiness we may realize the need to draw near the fount of life in all humility and trust and to be nourished with your word, Father, and with the body of Christ, invoking light, love, and mercy, for all men and women.

Ven. James Alberione

Eternal Father, open your gates today to the most miserable of your children, but one who greatly longs to see you.

Bd Jeanne Jugan

Show me, O Lord, your mercy, and delight my heart with it. Let me find you, whom I seek so longingly.

See: here is the man whom the robbers seized, and mishandled, and left half dead on the road to Jericho. O you who can what the kind-hearted Samaritan cannot: Come to my aid!

I am the sheep who wandered into the wilderness: Seek after me, and bring me home again to your fold. Do with me what you will, that all the days of my life I may bide by you, and praise you, with all those who are in heaven with you for all of eternity. Amen.

St Jerome

O Jesus my Saviour, see me prostrate at your feet. I adore, I bless and love your divine providence with all my heart for everything you will order in the future or permit about my person or about things concerning me; for your orders and permissions are equally admirable and lovable. Yes, my saviour, your holy will be done by all and through all, in spite of any repugnance in my heart. Your divine decrees and ordinances shall be blessed and glorified in all eternity.

I realize and confess, O my God, before heaven and earth, that you are just and that I observe these sufferings, and a thousand times more, for the least of my sins. That is the reason why I will embrace this affliction with all my heart to the glory of your divine justice, in submission to your sacred will, in honour of the terrible sufferings you endured on earth, in satisfaction for my sins, in fulfilment of your plans that you have made about me, and as something that comes from your most amiable hands and from your heart, full of love for me.

Be blessed, O my Jesus, that you have graciously given me an opportunity of suffering for love of you. Let me partake, if it pleases you, of the love, the humility, the patience, the sweetness, and the charity with which you suffered; and give me the grace to bear all these sufferings for your honour and your pure love. Amen.

St John Eudes

Though I stand at the door of your temple, yet I cannot refrain from evil thoughts! But Christ my God!—you who justified the publican, and who opened the very gate of paradise to the robber: open to me the source of your loving kindness. O, receive me, who comes to you, who would touch you, as you received the harlot, and her who had the unstoppable bleeding: for the one, touching but the hem of your garment, was straightaway made whole; embracing your undefiled feet, the other went away released from her sins. And I, vile sinner, am now bold enough to receive your whole body. Yet let me not be consumed; even as those others, receive me. Enlighten my spirit's senses, consume only the guilt of my sins—

At the prayers of the heavenly hosts—

At the prayers of her who, without seed, gave birth to you, who always are blessed. Amen.

St John of Damascus

O Lord, my love, if you are still mindful of my sins, and will not grant my petitions, your will be done, for that is my chief desire. Show your goodness and mercy, and you shall be known by them. If it be that you are waiting for my good works that in them you may grant my petition, do give them and work them in me: send also the penalties that you will accept, and do inflict them. But if you are not waiting for my good works, for what are you waiting, O most merciful Lord? why do you tarry? For if at last it must be grace and mercy, for which I pray in your Son, do accept my worthless offering, according to your will, and give me this good also according to your will. O Lord Almighty, my spirit has fainted within me because it has forgotten to feed upon you. I knew you not, O my Lord, when I went after vanity.

Who can free himself from base and mean ways, if you, O my God, will not lift him up to yourself in pure love? You hasten joyfully and lovingly, O Lord, to raise up him who has offended you, but I make no haste to honour and raise him up who has offended me. How shall a man raise himself up to you, for he is born and bred in misery, if you will not lift him up with the hand that made him? O Lord Almighty, if the shadow of the power of your justice in earthly sovereigns who govern and rule the nations can do so much, what cannot your almighty justice do, dealing with the just man and the sinner?

O Lord my God, you are not estranged from him who does not estrange himself from you. How is it that men say you are absent? O Lord my God, who is there that seeks you in pure and true love, who does not find you to be the joy of his will? It is you who are the first to show yourself, going forth to meet those who desire to meet you. You will not take away from me, O my God, what you have given me in your only-begotten Son Jesus Christ, in whom you have given me all I desire. I will, therefore, rejoice, you will not tarry if I wait for you. Wait in hope then, O my soul, for from henceforth you may love God in your heart.

The heavens are mine, the earth is mine, and the nations are mine: mine are the just, and the sinners are mine; mine are the angels, and the Mother of God; all things are mine, God himself is mine and for me, because Christ is mine, and all for me. For what do you then ask, for what do you seek, O my soul? All is yours, all is for you; do not take less, nor rest with the crumbs that fall from the table of your Father. Go forth and exult in your glory, hide yourself in it, and rejoice, and you shall obtain all the desires of your heart.

O sweetest love of God, too little known; he who has found you is at rest; let everything change, O my God, that we may rest in you. Everywhere with you, O my God, everywhere all

things with you as I wish. O my Love, all for you, nothing for
me; nothing for you, everything for me. All sweetness and
delight for you, none for me: all bitterness and trouble for me,
none for you. O my God, how sweet to me your presence,
who are the sovereign good. I will draw near to you in silence,
and will uncover your feet, that it may please you to unite me
to yourself, making my soul your bride: I will rejoice in
nothing till I am in your arms. O Lord, I beseech you, leave
me not for a moment, because I know not the value of my
soul.

St John of the Cross

The sins of my entire life, by which I have so often offended
you, my God, weigh me down like a mountain of my own
making. I wonder, 'What will be the end of all this?' Yet, I do
not lose hope.

I cannot bear this alone; I know I am weak. But your
strength will keep me from falling. The prayers of others will
uphold me in my time of need. I cannot repay such mercy; to
offer my life is only right.

Bd John Ri

O most adorable Trinity, Father, Son, and Holy Spirit, my God,
worthy of all my love, I prostrate myself before you. Mercifully
regard a most miserable sinner who would gladly be
reconciled to you by a good confession. But, O my God, as I
can do nothing if not aided by you, I implore you by the
compassion of your tender mercy to enlighten me, that I may
know all my sins: make me understand all their malice and

hideousness that I may detest them with my whole heart. O
Jesus, never-failing fountain of compassion, I approach you,
that you may cleanse me from all my iniquities. Sun of
righteousness, send the bright beams of your divine grace into
the dark recesses of my soul. Divine physician, heal your
infirm creature. O infinite love, enkindle the flames of your
love in my soul that it may love nothing but you. And may
this confession I am going to make be all that you would wish
it. May it bring about in me an entire change of life, so that I
may be fully reconciled to you, my God, my hope, my love;
for you are my saviour, and without you there is no peace for
my erring soul.

St Leonard

My God! I have had I know not what fresh light concerning a
love, which should be no common one, which you ask of
souls whom you have chosen to show forth the purity of your
love upon earth. Behold us! few in number, can we aim at
these heights? It seems to me we have this idea strongly in our
hearts; but the knowledge of our weakness, of our past
infidelities, makes us fear that you will repel us. Nevertheless,
the knowledge that you have put no limit to the number of
times that we should forgive makes us hope that you will treat
us in the same manner; and since it is so we believe in your
love for us. Since, O God, you have given us your Son, you
must love us, and we also are persuaded that we love
you….Behold us then, O saviour of mankind, at the foot of
your cross, fulfilling those words of yours: 'When I shall be
lifted up I will draw all men to myself.'

St Louise de Marillac

O my Jesus, you teach me from your cross the feelings of love and forbearance that I should have for my neighbour, and the service that you would have me render to them....What were your first words after the torments of the night and of the day of your bitter passion? They were words of deepest forbearance. 'Father, forgive them, they know not what they do!' My Jesus, infinite goodness, you did perceive that the passions of your enemies clouded their judgments and was the cause of their ignorance. What a lesson to us to teach us the forbearance with which we should forgive those who have injured us!

St Louise de Marillac

Lord Jesus Christ, Son of the living God, have mercy on me, a sinner.

St Macarius

Most sacred and divine heart of Jesus: Convinced of my unworthiness, I prostrate myself before you, to do you homage, to adore, love, and praise you as much as in my power.

O Jesus, my most sincere friend: I expose to you all my wants. I discover to you all my miseries, my weakness, my tepidity and sloth—in a word, all the wounds of my soul, and fervently implore you to let yourself be moved to pity by them, and come to my aid according to the magnitude of your mercies.

St Margaret Mary Alacoque

O sacred heart of Jesus: I fly to you, I unite myself with you, I enclose myself to you! Receive my call for help, O my saviour, as a sign of my horror of all within me contrary to your holy love. Let me rather die a thousand times than consent! Be my strength, O God: defend me, protect me. I am yours and desire forever to be yours!

St Margaret Mary Alacoque

Forgive us, most loving Father!

St Maria Soledad Torres Acosta

O my good master, to give you proof of my gratitude and to make reparation for my guilty life, I give you my heart and consecrate myself irrevocably and entirely to you. It is in your heart that I want to breathe, in your heart that I want to love.

O heart of Jesus, let my heart be the altar of your love and let it be ready for any sacrifice.

O my sweet Jesus, I give you my heart in thanksgiving for all your goodness. I consecrate myself entirely to you in reparation for my past unfaithfulness, and I resolve, with the help of your grace, never to offend you again.

Bd Mary of Providence

...O Lord, I seek of you to be allowed to depart. I have seen your salvation: let me be delivered from the bent yoke of the letter. I have seen the King Eternal, to whom no other succeeds: let me be set free from this servile and burdensome chain. I have seen him who is by nature my Lord and deliverer: may I obtain, then, his decree for deliverance. Set

me free from the yoke of condemnation, and place me under
the yoke of justification. Deliver me from the yoke of the
curse, and of the letter that kills, and enrol me in the blessed
company of those who, by the grace of this, your true Son,
who is of equal glory and power with you, have been received
into the adoption of sons.

St Methodius

Have mercy, Lord, on all my friends and relatives, on all my
benefactors, on all who pray to you for me, and on all who
have asked me to pray for them. Give them the spirit of
fruitful penance; mortify in them all vices, and make them
flower in all your virtues.

St Peter Damian

O Jesus, my Lord and my God, in you have I believed, you
have I loved, you have I sought all my life, you have I
announced and preached. A weak creature, I have sometimes
wandered from your ways. I ask pardon of you, my redeemer,
my glory, my crown; of you who will speedily wash me from
all my iniquities. Come to me, then, O Lord, to enable me to
go to you: receive me that I may receive you; and grant me
that I may dwell with you for ever and ever.

St Philip Benizi

O most sweet Jesus, who came into this world to give to all
souls the life of your grace, and who, to preserve and increase
it in them, willed to be the daily remedy of their weakness and
the food for each day, we humbly beseech you, by your heart

so burning with love for us, to pour your divine Spirit upon all souls in order that those who have the misfortune to be in the state of mortal sin may, returning to you, find the life of grace that they have lost.

Through this same Holy Spirit, may those who are already living by this divine life devoutly approach your divine table every day when it is possible, so that, receiving each day in Holy Communion the antidote of their daily venial sins and each day sustaining in themselves the life of your grace and thus ever purifying themselves the more, they may finally come to a happy life with you. Amen.

St Pius X

O Lord: If we compare before your eyes the punishment imposed upon us and the faults committed by us, it is less what we suffer and more what we deserve. We feel the penalty of sin, but we do not change the obstinacy of the sinner. Under your chastisement, our frailty breaks down, but we adhere to our wickedness. Our sick souls are tormented, but our necks are not bent. Our life is mourning in grief, but does not become better in works. If you pardon us, we fall again. At the time of punishment, we confess our faults. But if you are kind to us, we forget the cause of our tears. If your hand is upon us, we promise to do your will, but if you sheathe the sword, we forget what we have promised. If you strike, we implore your mercy, but if you treat us with forbearance, we provoke again your wrath. If distress has come over us, we implore you to grant us time for penance. If you show us your mercy, we presume upon your kindness that has spared us. If the inflicted punishment has just left us, our ungrateful mind

already has forgotten what it had to suffer. If you grant our
request quickly, we become impudent on account of your
leniency. If you are slow in listening to our prayers, we
complain impatiently of providence.

We confess, O Lord, our sins before you. Have mercy on us,
in your great clemency. We know that we deserve your
punishments. You are full of commiseration and forgiveness.
Grant us without our merits what we ask from you, who made
out of nothing those who might implore you. We cry to you,
O God: have mercy on us! Save us, O Lord our God, and
deliver us from all evil, that we, who wish to be rescued by
your gift, may enjoy faith and peace of all people in the
communion of eternal salvation, and in the delight of love.

St Prudentius

My sins, O Lord, do over-charge thy breast,
The weight thereof do force thy knees to bow;
Yea, flat thou fallest with my faults oppressed,
And bloody sweat runs trickling from thy brow:
But had they not to earth thus pressed thee,
Much more they would in hell have pressed me.

St Robert Southwell

Lord of all created things, my God, my blessedness: How long
must I yet wait before you show yourself to me? How can one
who has nothing on earth find life apart from you? How
tedious and how full of sufferings is such a life in which one
does not really live but experiences on every side utter
abandonment, utter desolation! How long, O Lord, ah, how

long will it yet last? What must I do, my highest good? Must I desire, really, never to yearn for you?

My God and my creator: You wound, but you also offer the means of healing. You wound, yet there can be seen no wound. You slay, and you grant life anew. In your omnipotence, according to your goodwill, you arrange everything, O Lord.

My God, do you will then that I, contemptible creature that I am, should endure such tribulation? So be it, then, my God, since you will it, for my will is no other, none, than yours. But O, my creator! the excess of my pain drives me to cry out and bewail my helplessness: be it your good pleasure to relieve me.

The fettered soul yearns for freedom, but wills it no sooner than it pleases you. My soul: let then the will of God be accomplished in you: alone, that concerns you. Serve the Lord, trust in his mercy: this will soothe your pains.

O my God, my King!—I can do nothing, unless your mighty hand, unless your heavenly power, assist me.

With your aid, I can do all.

St Teresa of Ávila

Open, my Jesus, your book of life wherein are recorded the actions of all the saints; those actions—would that I too had accomplished such for you!

St Thérèse of Lisieux

To you, O God, the fountain of mercy, I, a sinner, draw near. From my uncleanness, therefore, cleanse me. Enlighten my blindness, O sun of justice; heal my wounds, O eternal physician. King of kings, clothe my nakedness; mediator between God and man, take away my guilt. Have pity, O God, on my misery; pardon my crimes; restore to me life for death, virtue for impiety, and to my obduracy apply your saving grace.

O most clement Lord, call me back when I forget you, nor forsake me when I resist you. Raise me up when I fall, support me when I have risen, and guide me when I walk. Do not forget me when I forget you, nor forsake me when I forsake you. Despise me not in the midst of my sins. By sinning I have offended you, my God. I have injured my neighbour, and I have wounded myself.

By my weakness, O my God, I have sinned against you, the Father Almighty; by ignorance against you, O Son, supreme wisdom; by malice against you, O Holy Spirit, most clement. Thus I have offended you, most sublime Trinity. Alas for my misery how many and how great have been my sins. I have abandoned you, O Lord; I have murmured against you, O Lord; I have murmured against your goodness; and when confronted by evil love and evil fear, I have preferred rather to lose you than to forego the things that allure; rather to offend you than to incur the things that I fear. O my God, how far I have gone astray in word and deed. I have sinned obstinately in secret and in public. Hence, I beseech you that because of my weakness you will not regard my iniquity, but your own immense goodness, and bestowing upon me sorrow for the past and caution for the future, you will mercifully forgive all the evil that I have done.

St Thomas Aquinas

Give me thy grace, good Lord, to set the world at naught; to set my mind fast upon thee; and not to hang upon the blast of men's mouths.

To be content to be solitary; not to long for worldly company; little and little utterly to cast off the world, and rid my mind of all the business thereof; not to long to hear of any worldly things, but that the hearing of worldly phantasies may be to me displeasant.

Gladly to be thinking of God; piteously to call for his help; to lean unto the comfort of God; busily to labour to love him.

To know mine own vility and wretchedness; to humble and meeken myself under the mighty hand of God. To bewail my sins past; for the purging of them patiently to suffer adversity; gladly to bear my purgatory here; to be joyful of tribulations; to walk the narrow way that leadeth to life.

To bear the cross with Christ; to have the last things in remembrance; to have ever afore mine eye my death that is ever at hand; to make death no stranger to me; to foresee and consider the everlasting fire of hell; to pray for pardon before the Judge come.

To have continually in mind that passion that Christ suffered for me; for his benefits uncessantly to give him thanks.

To buy the time again, that I before have lost; to abstain from vain confabulations; to eschew light, foolish mirth and gladness; recreations not necessary to cut off; of worldly substance, friends, liberty, life, and all, to set the loss at right naught for the winning of Christ.

To think my most enemies my best friends; for the brethren of Joseph could never have done him so much good with their love and favour as they did him with their malice and hatred.

These minds are more to be desired of every man than all the treasure of all the princes and kings, Christian and heathen, were it gathered and laid together all upon one heap.

St Thomas More

Now, good gracious Lord, as thou givest me thy grace to knowledge [my sins], so give me thy grace not only in word but in heart also, with very sorrowful contrition to repent them and utterly to forsake them. And forgive me those sins also in which, by mine own default, through evil affections and evil custom, my reason is with sensuality so blinded that I cannot discern them for sin. And illumine, good Lord, mine heart, and give me thy grace to know them and to knowledge them, and forgive me my sins negligently forgotten, and bring them to my mind with grace to be purely confessed of them.

St Thomas More

Have mercy on me, O God; and hear my prayer.

Have mercy on me, O Lord, for I am weak: heal me, O Lord, for my bones are troubled.

Have mercy on me, O Lord; see my humiliation that I suffer from my enemies.

Have mercy on me, O Lord, for I am afflicted: my eye is troubled with wrath, my soul, and my belly.

Have mercy on me, O God, according to your great mercy.

Have mercy on me, O God, for man has trodden me under foot: all the day long he has afflicted me, fighting against me.

Have mercy on me, O God, have mercy on me: for my soul trusts in you.

Have mercy on me, O Lord, for I have cried to you all the day.
Give joy to the soul of your servant, for to you, O Lord, I have
lifted up my soul.
Have mercy on us, O Lord, have mercy on us: for we are greatly
filled with contempt.

Glory be to the Father, and to the Son, and to the Holy Spirit: As
it was in the beginning, is now, and ever shall be, world without
end. Amen.

St Vincent Ferrer

Pardon us, O Lord, pardon us. We beg to shift the blame for
our sins, we make excuses. But no one can hide himself from
the light of your truth, which both enlightens those who turn
to it, and exposes those who turn away. Even our blood and
our bones are visible to you, who created us out of dust.

How foolish we are to think that we can rule our own lives,
satisfying our own desires, without thought of you. How
stupid we are to imagine that we can keep our sins hidden.
But although we may deceive other people, we cannot deceive
you. And since you see into our hearts, we cannot deceive
ourselves, for your light reveals to us our own spiritual
corruption.

Let us, therefore, fall down before you, weeping with tears
of shame. May your judgment give new shape to our souls.
May your power mould our hearts to reflect your love. May
your grace infuse our minds, so that our thoughts reflect your
will.

Bd William of Saint Thierry

PRAYERS
OF
PETITION

Almighty God, Father of our Lord Jesus Christ, grant, we pray, that we might be grounded and settled in your truth by the coming of your Holy Spirit into our hearts. What we do not know, reveal to us; what is lacking within us, make complete; that which we do know, confirm in us; and keep us blameless in your service, through Jesus Christ our Lord.

St Clement of Rome

God of mercy, hear the prayer that I offer for your people....
...O Lord my God, hear me, and let your eyes be open day and night upon them. Spread your wings and protect them in your goodness, extend your holy power and bless them, pour your Holy Spirit into their hearts, and may he keep them in unity of spirit and in the bond of peace, chaste in body and humble of heart. May your good Spirit dwell in their thoughts so that in his light they may come to know you. May they impress on themselves the remembrance of him on whom they should call in trouble and consult in doubt. May this gentle comforter come to the aid of all those who are grieved by temptation, and may he strengthen their weakness among the trials and difficulties of this life.

Moved by your Spirit, dear Lord, may they be at peace with one another, in themselves and with me....Be in the midst of them according to your solemn promise. And since you know the need of each one, I beseech you to strengthen the feeble, not to cast out the weak, to cure the sick, comfort the sorrowful, revive the weary, confirm the wavering, and may all find the help of your grace in their needs and temptations....

I place them in your holy hands and commit them to your loving providence; may no one snatch them from your hand....May they persevere joyfully in their holy resolve, and in persevering may they attain to eternal life, through your help, dear Lord, you who are living and reigning through all the ages. Amen.

St Aelred of Rievaulx

Eternal Father, for the love of Jesus Christ, let me never fail to recommend myself to you whenever I am tempted. I know you always help me when I have recourse to you; but my fear is that I may forget to recommend myself to you, and so my negligence will be the cause of my ruin. By the merits of Jesus Christ, give me grace to pray to you. But grant me such an abundant grace that I may always pray, and pray as I ought!

St Alphonsus de' Liguori

Dear Lord, I am now convinced that without patient suffering I cannot merit a reward in heaven. It is you who must give me patience in suffering. I make the resolution to accept with patience all the trials and sufferings that will come into my life. I know that so often, in spite of my resolutions, I have become despondent when I was asked to carry a cross; but if I do not learn to suffer for love of you, I shall suffer without merit. My Jesus, by the merits of the patience with which you suffered so many pains for love of me, give me the grace to bear my crosses for love of you.

St Alphonsus de' Liguori

O God of love, you are and shall be forever the only delight of my heart and the sole object of my affections.

Since Jesus said, 'Ask and you shall receive,' I do not hesitate to say, 'Give me your love and your grace.'

Grant that I may love you and be loved by you. I want nothing else.

St Alphonsus de' Liguori

I do love you, my sovereign good; I love you with all my heart;
I love you more than myself; I love you, and I want to do
nothing but love you.

I see that this goodwill of mine is entirely the gift of your
grace; but, my Lord, finish the work, help me always till I die.
Don't leave me in my own hands; give me strength to
overcome temptations and to conquer myself; and so make me
always commend myself to you.

I want to be all yours; I give you my body, my soul, my
will, and my freedom; I no longer want to live for myself, but
only for you, my creator, my redeemer, my love, my
everything: my God and my all. I want to become a saint, and
I hope for this from you.

Afflict me as you will, deprive me of everything, so long as
you don't deprive me of your grace and your love.

St Alphonsus de' Liguori

Most amiable heart of my divine saviour, heart in love with
men, heart loving us with such great tenderness, heart worthy
to reign over our hearts and to possess them entirely, help me
to understand more clearly how much you love me and all the
souls in the world. My Jesus, please accept the offering and the
sacrifice that I make to you this day as I once more sincerely
offer to you my entire will. Tell me what you want me to do.
Your holy grace will help me do it.

St Alphonsus de' Liguori

O my God, up to now I have not thought too much about death, I have not looked into its face. And perhaps this is why I have offended you too much and have not loved you enough. But now I firmly resolve to serve you in earnest. Give me, O Lord, the strength to do so. Do not abandon me. You did not abandon me when I offended you; I, therefore, hope more confidently for your help now that I propose to serve you more faithfully.

St Alphonsus de' Liguori

My Jesus, you have taught me this prayer: Thy kingdom come! Lord, I do now pray that your kingdom may come into my heart, so that you may possess it entirely, and that I may possess you forever!

You have spared nothing to save me and win my love; take me then, and let my salvation consist in loving you always in this life and in the next. Keep your hand upon me that I may never more offend you.

St Alphonsus de' Liguori

Lovable Lord, let your holy love come possess me completely: let it reign and rule in this heart of mine that for an unhappy time rebelled against you. Lovable Lord, possess me.

O divine love that makes happy the souls you ignite with heavenly flames, O come to my heart, and make it worthy of your pure love: set it on fire. Ah, divine love, consume me.

St Alphonsus de' Liguori

O God, you are so lovable and worthy of infinite love. How can you bear that so many people in this world whom you have showered with gifts refuse to know and love you? They even offend and despise you.

Most loving God, may your name be adored and loved by all people throughout the world. I beg you, do not let me leave you without your granting some grace for those on whose behalf I am praying.

St Alphonsus de' Liguori

Jesus Christ, my God, I adore you and I thank you for the many favours you have bestowed on me this day. I offer you my sleep and all the moments of this night, and I pray you to preserve me from sin. Therefore, I place myself in your most sacred side, and under the mantle of our blessed Lady my Mother. May the holy angels assist me and keep me in peace, and may your blessing be upon me.

St Alphonsus de' Liguori

My Jesus, you have sacrificed yourself and have died for me. But how have I repaid your love? I thank you for having had so much patience with me and for giving me time to repair my ingratitude. I am sorry, my saviour, and from now on I wish to do whatever is pleasing to you. I accept now the death you wish to send me, with all the pains and sufferings that may accompany it. Grant that during life I may be resigned to the arrangements of your divine providence and that, when death comes, I may accept your holy will. I wish to die saying: 'Your will be done.'

St Alphonsus de' Liguori

O Lord our God: Grant us grace to desire you with our whole hearts, that, desiring, we may seek and find you; so finding you, that we may love you; so in loving you, that we may hate those sins from which you have redeemed us, for the sake of Jesus Christ. Amen.

St Anselm of Canterbury

O holy Paraclete! sweetest consolation of the sorrowful! gracious Spirit! O come down with your mighty power into the deep recesses of our hearts! Lighten there with your brightness every dark retreat, enrich all with the dew of your abundant comfort! Kindle our inward parts with holy fervour, that the incense of our prayers and praises may always go up to you, O our God—through Jesus Christ, your Son, our Lord. Amen.

St Anselm of Canterbury

I beseech you, O my God, that I may know you, love you, and rejoice in you. If in this life I cannot do these things fully, grant that I may at the least progress in them from day to day. Advance in me the knowledge of you now, that in the life to come it may be complete. Increase in me the love of you here, that there it may be full. O God of truth: I pray that I may obtain that which you promise, that my joy may be made full. And in the meantime, let my mind meditate on it; let my soul hunger after it, and my whole being long for it, till at last I enter into the joy of my Lord, who is God, blessed forever. Amen.

St Anselm of Canterbury

O God! You are the life, wisdom, truth, bounty, and
blessedness, eternal, the true and only good! My God, my
Lord: you are my hope and my heart's joy. With thanksgiving,
I confess that you made me in your own image, that I may
direct all my thoughts to you and love you. Lord, make me
know you aright, that I may love you more and more, and
enjoy, and even possess you! And since, in this life, here, on
earth, I cannot attain this blessedness most fully, let it at least,
day by day, take growth in me, until all be fulfilled in
everlasting life, long at last. Here, let my love toward you and
in you grow: there, let it ripen—that you, my joy, being here
great in hope, may there be made perfect fruits. Amen.

St Anselm of Canterbury

We love you, O God, and desire to love you more and more.
Grant that we may love you as we wish to love you and as we
should love you. O dearest friend, you who have loved us so
deeply and redeemed us; come and take your place in our
hearts. Watch over our lips, our steps, and our deeds and we
need no longer fear for soul and body.

Yes, give us love, most precious of gifts, which knows no
enemies. Give our hearts that pure love borne on your love for
us, that we may love others as you love us. O most loving
Father of Jesus Christ from whom all love flows, grant that our
hearts, frozen in sin and grown cold toward you, may be
warmed in the divine glow. Help and bless us in your Son.

O blessed Lord, you have commanded us to love one
another; give us the grace that, as we have received your

unmerited favours, we may love all persons in you and for you. We implore your clemency for all people, but particularly for our friends whom you have given us. Love them, Source of Love, and instill in them a thorough love of yourself, that they may seek, utter, and do nothing save what is pleasing to you. Amen.

St Anselm of Canterbury

Father, give me humility, meekness, chastity, patience, and charity.

Father, teach me goodness, knowledge, and discipline.

Father, give me your love together with your grace and I will be rich enough.

My God, my Jesus, and my all!

St Anthony Mary Claret

O Jesus and Mary, the love I have for you makes me desire death so as to be united to you in heaven. But my love is so great that it makes me plead for a long life, so as to gain souls for heaven. O love, O love, O love!

St Anthony Mary Claret

We beseech you, O heavenly Father, through our Lord Jesus Christ, whom you have made 'the sacrifice that takes our sins away' [1 John 4:10], to receive through him our offerings and prayers, and through him give us the grace to be reconciled to you and to our brothers here on earth, and being thus at peace with you and with them, to offer our sacrifices of praise with the holy angels before your golden altar in the Jerusalem that is above. This we ask of you who, three in one, are blessed forever!

St Anthony of Padua

May the darkness of sin and the night of unbelief vanish before the light of the word and the Spirit of grace. And may the heart of Jesus live in the hearts of all people. Amen.

Bd Arnold Janssen

May the holy triune God live in our hearts and in the hearts of all people. Amen.

Bd Arnold Janssen

O holy, unspeakable, wonderful, and mighty God!—whose power and whose wisdom have no end, before whom all powers tremble and adore, at whose glance the heavens and the very earth flee away, O you are love; you are my Father: I will love and worship you for evermore.

You have shown me pity. From your light, a ray has shone upon my inward eye: Guide me into the perfect light, that it may illumine me, wholly, and that all darkness may flee away! Let the holy flame of your love so burn in all my heart that it may be made pure, and I may see you, O Lord, for it is the pure in heart who see you.

You have set me free; you have drawn me to you: therefore, do not forsake me, but keep me always in your grace. Guide me, and rule me. Perfect me for your kingdom, Lord. Amen.

St Augustine

O Lord our God, 'under the shadow of your wings let us hope'; protect us, and carry us. You will carry us both when little, and 'even to hoar hairs will you carry us'; for our firmness, when it is you, then is it firmness; but when our own, it is infirmity. Our good ever lives with you; from which when we turn away, we are turned aside. Let us now, O Lord, return, that we may not be overturned, because with you our good lives without any decay, which good you are; nor need we fear, lest there be no place whither to return, because we fell from it: for through our absence, our mansion fell not—your eternity.

St Augustine

Blessed are all your saints, my God and King! who have through travail and in peace of soul all travelled within the ship with you, the tempestuous sea of mortality, and have, at last, made the desired port of peace and of felicity!

O, cast a gracious eye upon us who are in our dangerous voyage still! Remember, succour us in our distress: think of those who lie exposed to the rough storms of troubles and temptations! Strengthen our weakness in your strength, that valiantly we may do your will in this spiritual battle. Help us against our own negligence, our cowardice: defend us from the treachery of our unfaithful hearts. We are exceedingly frail, and indisposed to every virtuous and gallant undertaking. Grant, O Lord, that we may bring our vessel safe to shore, into our desired haven, Lord. Amen.

St Augustine

O! that I might repose in you! O! that you would enter into my heart, and inebriate it, that I may forget my ills, and embrace you, my sole good. What are you to me? In your pity, teach me to utter it. Or what am I to you that you demand my love, and, if I give it not, are wroth with me, and threaten me with grievous woes? Is it then a slight woe to love you not? O! for your mercies' sake, tell me, O Lord my God, what you are to me. Say to my soul, 'I am your salvation.' So speak, that I may hear. Behold, Lord, my heart is before you; open my ears, and say to my soul, 'I am your salvation.' After this voice let me haste, and take hold of you. Hide not your face from me. Let me die—lest I die— only let me see your face.

St Augustine

Lord Jesus, may I know myself and know you,
    And desire nothing save only you.

May I hate myself and love you.
May I do everything for the sake of you.
May I humble myself and exalt you.
May I think of nothing except you.
May I die to myself and live in you.
May I receive whatever happens as from you.
May I banish self and follow you,
    And ever desire to follow you.
May I fly from myself and fly to you,
    That I may deserve to be defended by you.
May I fear for myself and fear you,
    And be among those who are chosen by you.
May I distrust myself and trust in you.
May I be willing to obey on account of you.

May I cling to nothing but to you.
May I be poor for the sake of you.

Look upon me that I may love you.
Call me that I may see you,
    And ever and ever enjoy you. Amen.

St Augustine

Cleanse me, O Lord, in this life, so that I may not require to pass through that purification designed for those who shall be saved yet so as by fire.

St Augustine

Be mindful, O Lord, of all sovereignty and authority and of those who exercise them. Keep the good according to your goodness; make good those who are evil, according to your loving-kindness.

St Basil the Great

O Lord our God, teach us, we beseech you, to ask for the gift we need. Steer the ship of our life to yourself, the quiet harbour of all storm-stressed souls.

Show us the course that we are to take. Renew in us the spirit of docility. Let your Spirit curb our fickleness; guide and strengthen us to perform what is for our own good, to keep your commandments, and ever to rejoice in your glorious and vivifying presence. Yours is the glory and praise for all eternity. Amen.

St Basil the Great

O Christ our God, in all times and places you are worshipped and glorified both in heaven and on earth. You are long-suffering and generous in your mercy and compassion. You love the just and show mercy to the sinner, calling all people to repentance through the promise to come. O Lord, at this very hour, receive our supplications and direct our lives in the path of your commandments. Sanctify our souls; purify our bodies; set aright our minds; cleanse our thoughts; deliver us from all affliction, trouble, and distress; surround us with your holy angels so that, guided and guarded in their camp, we may attain oneness of faith and the knowledge of your unspeakable glory. For you are blessed forever and ever. Amen.

St Basil the Great

O Christ, our Master and God, King of the ages and creator of all, I thank you for all the good things that you have given to me and for the reception of your most pure and life-giving mysteries. I pray you, therefore, O good lover of humanity, keep me under your protection in the shadow of your wings. Grant that with a pure conscience, until my last breath, I may worthily partake of your holy things, for the forgiveness of sins and for life everlasting. For you are the bread of life, the fountain of holiness, and the bestower of blessings, and to you we give glory together with the Father and the Holy Spirit, now and for ever and ever. Amen.

St Basil the Great

Bestow upon me, O gracious, O holy Father:
Intellect to understand you,
Perceptions to perceive you purely,
Reason to discern you,
Diligence to seek you,
Wisdom to find you,
A spirit to know you;

A heart to meditate upon you,
Ears to hear you,
Eyes to behold you,
A tongue to proclaim you,
A conversation pleasing to you,
Patience to wait for you,
And perseverance to look for you.

Grant me a perfect end—your holy presence.

Grant me a blessed resurrection, and your recompense,
everlasting life. Amen.

St Benedict

O my Lord! if I may not shed my blood, and may not give my
life for you, let me at least, O Lord, die to all that is displeasing
to you!

St Bernadette Soubirous of Lourdes

O Jesus! I implore you: Give to me the bread of patience, and
support the grief that tortures my heart.

St Bernadette Soubirous of Lourdes

O Jesus! make me realize more fully the jealousy of divine love! Detach my affections from the creature; raise them up and bind them to yourself!

St Bernadette Soubirous of Lourdes

O Jesus, give me, I pray
    the bread of humility,
    the bread of obedience,
    the bread of charity,
    the bread of patience to bear the sufferings of my poor heart....

O Jesus, you want me to be crucified; *fiat!*

Give me
    the bread of strength to suffer as I ought,
    the bread of seeing only you in all things and always.

Jesus,
Mary,
The Cross:
    I want no other friends but these.

St Bernadette Soubirous of Lourdes

Saturday

O Jesus, Love most joyful and most glorious! when shall I be wholly inebriated with you? When shall I be visibly inebriated with you? When shall I be so joined to you that I offend you in nothing, and am unable to be severed from you? How long shall I be removed from your face? To be without you is a continual grief to me, and like eternal death. O most sweet

Jesus! I worship your glorious name and commend myself to you.

Sunday
O good Jesus: Make me love you ardently!

Monday
Jesus, sweet Love: Make me feel with what unbounded love you have loved us, and still do love us!

Tuesday
Most loving Jesus, I would love you, but without you, I cannot.

Wednesday
Jesus, my love: Make me die for love of you!

Thursday
Jesus, my love: Grant me fervent love to you, humble obedience, and thanksgiving; that is, let me have a continual sense of your benefits and of praising and blessing you!

Friday
O my Jesus! crucified for me: Empty yourself into me and fasten yourself to me with the nails of your love!

St Bernardine of Siena

O Lord Jesus, acknowledge what is yours in us, and take away from us all that is not yours; for your honour and glory. Amen.

St Bernardine of Siena

O Lord Jesus Christ, son of the living God, receive this prayer
in that most exceeding love, with which you bore all the
wounds of your most sacred body; and remember me, your
servant, and to all sinners, and all the faithful, living and dead,
give mercy, grace, remission, and eternal life. Amen.

St Birgitta

O sweetest Lord, Jesus Christ: I beseech you, pierce the inmost
marrow of my soul with the tender and lifegiving wound of
your love, with true and calm apostolic charity, so that my
whole soul may always languish, may always faint for love of
you, always for desire of you, always for you alone! May my
soul long for you: may it pine for you in the courts of your
house! May my soul desire to be dissolved in you and to be
with you!

Bread of angels: Grant that my soul may hunger for you,
refreshment of holy souls, our daily bread, which has all
manner of savour and sweetness, all most holy delights; may
my heart always hunger for you, feasting on you, on whom
the angels long to look. May my inmost soul fill with the
sweetness of the taste of you, well of life: May it ever thirst for
you, fountain of wisdom, of knowledge, source of everlasting
life, torrent of pleasure, richness of abundance of the house of
God.

May my soul ever yearn toward you; may my soul seek you,
find you, tend toward attainment of you, always meditate on
you, always speak of you, and do all things to the praise and
glory of your name, with discretion, with humility, with love,
delighting; with ready care, with affection rejoicingly, with
perseverance to the end. You alone and evermore be my hope;

my whole trust wholly; my riches; my delight; my joy, rest, and tranquillity; my peace and my sweet contentment; my fragrance and my sweet; my food, my feast, and my refreshment; my refuge and my help; my wisdom, portion, possession; and my treasure, in whom my mind, my heart, may always remain fixed and firm, rooted immovably, for evermore. Amen.

St Bonaventure

Lord Jesus Christ, who came to this world as a man and suffered your passion, allowing your hands to be nailed to the cross for our sins, give me the strength to endure my passion.

St Boris of Kiev

O my sovereign Lord: you who increase all things: Bless, O God of unbounded greatness, this storehouse with your right hand.

My storehouse shall be a storehouse of bright testimony, the storehouse that my king shall bless, a storehouse in which plenty shall abound.

The Son of Mary, my beloved one, will bless my storehouse. His is the glory of the whole universe. May that glory ever be multiplied, and be given to him.

St Brigid

O Lord Jesus Christ! I adore you hanging on the cross, wearing on your head the crown of thorns: I implore you that your cross may deliver me from the blows of the angel of vengeance. *Our Father* and *Hail Mary*.

O Lord Jesus Christ! I adore you wounded on the cross,

given gall and vinegar to drink: I pray you that your wounds may be a cure for my soul. *Our Father* and *Hail Mary*.

O Lord Jesus Christ! by that bitterness that you suffered on the cross for my sins, especially at that moment when your most beautiful soul departed from your blessed body: I implore you, have pity on my soul when it departs from my body, lead it to eternal life. *Our Father* and *Hail Mary*.

O Lord Jesus Christ! I adore you descending into hell and delivering the captives: I implore you, do not permit me to enter there. *Our Father* and *Hail Mary*.

O Lord Jesus Christ! I adore you restored to life among the dead, ascending into heaven, and seating yourself at the right hand of your Father: I implore you to make me worthy to follow you there, and to be presented to you. *Our Father* and *Hail Mary*.

O Lord Jesus Christ, Good Shepherd! save the righteous, justify the sinners, have pity on all the faithful, and be merciful to me, a sinner. So be it. *Our Father* and *Hail Mary*.

O Lord Jesus Christ! I adore you laid in the sepulchre, embalmed with myrrh and spices: I implore you that your death may be my life. Amen. *Our Father* and *Hail Mary*.

St Catherine dei Ricci

Holy Spirit, come into my heart.
By your power, snatch it up to you, O God.
Give me love and holy fear.

Christ, save me from all evil desire.
Inflame and warm me with your most sweet love.
That way every burden will seem light.

I beg your care and help in need.
Christ, my Love. Christ, my Love.

St Catherine of Siena

Bestow on me, O Lord God, understanding to know you,
diligence to seek you, wisdom to find you, a perseverance in
waiting patiently for you, and a hope that may embrace you at
the last.

St Catherine of Siena

O eternal Trinity, I have known in your light, which came to
me with the light of holy faith, the many wonderful things you
have declared to me. You have set out for me the path of
supreme perfection, so that I no longer need serve you in
darkness, but in your splendid light, and so that I may be a
mirror of a good and holy life, arising from the darkness of my
sins. Self-love darkened the eye of my intellect, but you,
eternal Trinity, have dissipated the darkness with your light.

Clothe me, clothe me with yourself, O Eternal Truth, so
that I may run my mortal course with true obedience, my soul
inebriated with your light and your love.

St Catherine of Siena

Precious blood,
Ocean of divine mercy:
Flow upon us!

Precious blood,
Most pure offering:
Procure us every grace!

Precious blood,
Hope and refuge of sinners:
Atone for us!

Precious blood,
Delight of holy souls:
Draw us!
Amen.

St Catherine of Siena

O Father of Mercy, look into the face of your anointed one,
who pleads for his bride and our mother, the holy Church,
with a loud voice and tears. See, O my Father, the bloody
sweat, the terrible crown of thorns, the hands and feet that
have been pierced by nails, the wounds of our brother Jesus
Christ: hear, O Father, the sobs of your much beloved Son on
the cross. They have moved the heavens, split the rocks.
Should your mercy remain unmoved? Keep everyone who
recognizes you with a sincere heart within the holy faith,
protect everyone from false prophets who go about in sheep's
clothing but are ferocious wolves on the inside; keep their
power away so that their attacks may fail and they be

destroyed. Merciful God, grant to those who believe in you the grace to love you continually in unity and love, to follow you loyally into death, and there to praise and honour you forever.

St Clement Maria Hofbauer

Be gracious, O instructor, to us, your children—Father, charioteer of Israel, Son and Father, both in one, O Lord! Grant to us who obey your precepts that we may perfect the likeness of the Image, and with all our power know him who is the good God, and not a harsh judge. And do you yourself cause that all of us who have our conversation in your peace, who have been translated into your commonwealth, having sailed tranquilly over the billows of sin, may be wafted in calm by your Holy Spirit, by the ineffable wisdom, by night and by day, to the perfect day; and giving thanks may praise, and praising, thank the only Father and Son, Son and Father, the Son, instructor and teacher, with the Holy Spirit, all in one, in whom is all, for whom all is one, for whom is eternity, whose members we all are, whose glory the æons are, for the all-good, all-lovely, all-wise, all-just one: to whom be glory both now and forever. Amen.

St Clement of Alexandria

O God, make us children of quietness, and heirs of peace.

St Clement of Rome

Grant to us, Lord, that we may set our hope on your name which is the primal source of all creation. Open the eyes of our heart that we may know you, who alone are highest in the high, holy in the holy, who lay low the insolence of the proud, who scatter the imagination of the nations, who set the lowly on high and bring the lofty low, who make the rich and make the poor, who kill and make alive, who alone is the benefactor of spirits and the God of all flesh, who look into the abyss, who scan our works, the succour of those in peril, the saviour of those in despair, the creator and overseer of every spirit, who multiply the nations on earth and choose out from all those who love you through Jesus Christ, your beloved Son, through whom you did instruct us, sanctify us, honour us. We beseech you, Lord and master, be our help and succour, save those among us who are in tribulations, have mercy on the lowly, lift up the fallen, show yourself to the needy, heal the ungodly, convert the wanderers of your people, feed the hungry, release our prisoners, raise up the weak, comfort the fainthearted, let all nations know that you are God, you alone, with Jesus Christ, your Son, and we are your people, the sheep of your pasture.

St Clement of Rome

Be thou a bright flame before me,
Be thou a guiding star above me,
Be thou a smooth path below me,
Be thou a kindly shepherd behind me,
Today — tonight — and forever.

St Columba

Lord, I pray that you may be a lamp for me in the darkness. Touch my soul and kindle a fire within it, that it may burn brightly and give light to my life. Thus my body may truly become your temple, lit by your perpetual flame burning on the altar of my heart. And may the light within me shine on my brethren that it may drive away the darkness of ignorance and sin from them also. Thus together let us be lights to the world, manifesting the bright beauty of your gospel to all around us.

St Columbanus

I beseech you, merciful God, to allow me to drink from the stream that flows from your fountain of life. May I taste the sweet beauty of its waters, which spring from the very depths of your truth. O Lord, you are that fountain from which I desire with all my heart to drink. Give me, Lord Jesus, this water that it may quench the burning spiritual thirst within my soul, and purify me from all sin.

I know, King of glory, that I am asking from you a great gift. But you give to your faithful people without counting the cost, and you promise even greater things in the future. Indeed, nothing is greater than yourself, and you have given yourself to mankind on the cross. Therefore, in praying for the waters of life, I am praying that you, the source of those waters, will give yourself to me. You are my light, my salvation, my food, my drink, my God.

St Columbanus

I beg you, most loving saviour, to reveal yourself to us, that knowing you we may desire you, that desiring you we may love you, that loving you we may ever hold you in our thoughts.

St Columbanus

Grant, O God, that love and suffering may grow hand in hand in me, so that I may love you more and more with the cheerful disposition that is the fruit of love.

O Lord, only grant me love for you, and I shall be rich enough.

I desire only that you leave me to my nothingness and that you alone, if I may say so, be all in all and loved and honoured by everybody.

I wish to take pleasure in nothing but only in you and your love.

Bd Crescentia Höss

O God, who was and is, you willed that I should be born. You brought me to salvation through the waters of baptism. Be with me now and strengthen my soul that I will not weaken.

Praise to God who has looked upon me and delivered me from my enemies.

St Crispina

Good God, may we confess your name to the end; may we emerge unmarked and glorious from the traps and darkness of this world. As you have bound us together by charity and peace, and as together we have persevered under persecution, so may we also rejoice together in your heavenly kingdom.

St Cyprian of Carthage

O Lord, my God, you have created the choirs of angels and spiritual powers. You have stretched forth the heavens and established the earth, creating all that exists from nothing.

You hear those who obey your will and keep your commandments in holy fear. Hear my prayer and protect your faithful people. Keep them free from harm and the worldly cunning of those who blaspheme you.

Build up your Church and gather all into unity. Make your people known for the unity of their profession of faith. Inspire the hearts of your people with your word and teaching.

May all praise and glorify your name, the Father, Son, and Holy Spirit. Amen.

St Cyril

What blessing, or what praise, or what thanksgiving can we render to you, O God, lover of humanity, for when we were cast away by the doom of death, and drowned in the depth of sin, you granted us freedom, and bestowed on us this immortal, this heavenly food, and manifested to us this mystery, hid from ages and from generations? This, your supreme act of mercy, and the greatness of your benignity and fatherly care for us, grant us to understand. Amen.

St Cyril of Alexandria

Lord Christ, let me not be put to shame.

Christ, I beseech you, let me not be put to shame.

Christ, come to my aid, have pity upon me, let me not be put to shame.

Christ, I beseech you, give me the strength to suffer what I must for you.

St Dativus

Come, my light, and illumine my darkness.

Come, my life, and revive me from death.

Come, my physician, and heal my wounds.

Come, flame of divine love, and burn up the thorns of my sins, kindling my heart with the flame of your love.

Come, my King, sit upon the throne of my heart and reign there.

For you alone are my King and my Lord.

St Dimitrii of Rostov

O God the Father: origin of divinity, good beyond all that is good, fair beyond all that is fair, in whom is calmness, peace, concord: Heal the dissensions that divide us from one another, and bring us back into the unity of love that resembles your divine nature. As you are above all things, make us one by the unanimity of a good mind, that through the embrace of charity, and the bonds of godly affection, we may spiritually be one, as well in ourselves as in one another, by that peace of yours that makes all things peaceful. Through the grace, the mercy, and the tenderness of your only-begotten Son, Jesus, the Christ, our Lord.

St Dionysius of Alexandria

Bless the mind deeply troubled
Of the sufferers,
The heavy loneliness of profound souls
The restlessness of human beings,
The sorrow which no soul ever confides
To a sister soul.

And bless the passage of moths at night,
Who do not shun spectres on paths unknown.
Bless the distress of men
Who die within the hour,
Grant them, loving God, a peaceful, blessed end.

Bless all the hearts, the clouded ones, Lord, above all,
Bring healing to the sick.
To those in torture, peace.
Teach those who had to carry their beloved to the grave, to forget.
Leave none in agony of guilt on all the earth.

Bless the joyous ones, O Lord, and keep them under your wing.—
My mourning clothes you never yet removed.
At times my tired shoulders bear a heavy burden.
But give me strength, and I'll bear it
In penitence to the grave.

Then bless my sleep, the sleep of all the dead.
Remember what your son suffered for me in agony of death.
Your great mercy for all human needs
Give rest to all the dead in your eternal peace.

Bd Edith Stein

Into your hands, O Lord, and into the hands of your holy angels, I commit and entrust this day my soul, my relations, my benefactors, my friends, and my enemies, and all your Catholic people.

Keep us, O Lord, through the day, by the merits and intercession of the Blessed Virgin Mary and all your saints, from all vicious and unruly desires, from all sins and temptations of the devil, and from sudden and unprovided death and the pains of hell.

Illuminate my heart with the grace of the Holy Spirit; grant that I may ever be obedient to your commandments; suffer me not to be separated from you, O God, who live and reign with God the Father and the same Holy Spirit for ever and ever. Amen.

St Edmund Rich of Abingdon

Unite me to thyself, O adorable victim;
Life-giving heavenly bread, feed me;
Sanctify me, reign in me;
Transform me to thyself;
Live in me, let me live in thee;
Let me adore thee in thy life-giving
Sacraments as my God;
Listen to thee, as to my master;
Obey thee as my King;
Imitate thee as my model;
Follow thee as my shepherd;
Love thee as my Father;
Seek thee as my physician;
Who will heal all the maladies of my soul.

Be indeed my way, truth and life.
Sustain me, O heavenly manna
Through the desert of this world,
Till I shall behold thee unveiled in thy glory.

St Elizabeth Ann Bayley Seton
(Her paraphrase of the Anima Christi)

O my God, Trinity whom I adore
help me to forget myself entirely
that I may be established in you
as still and as peaceful
as if my soul were already in eternity.

May nothing trouble my peace
or make me leave you,
O my unchanging one,
but may each minute
carry me further
into the depths of your mystery.

Give peace to my soul,
make it your heaven,
your beloved dwelling
and your resting place.

May I never leave you there alone
but be wholly present,
my faith wholly vigilant,
wholly adoring,
and wholly surrendered to your creative action.

O my beloved Christ,
crucified by love,
I wish to be a bride for your heart;
I wish to cover you with glory;
I wish to love you…
even unto death!

But I feel my weakness,
and I ask you to 'clothe me with yourself,'
to identify my soul with all the movements of your Soul,
to overwhelm me,
to possess me,
to substitute yourself for me
that my life may be but a radiance of your life.

Come into me as adorer,
as restorer,
as saviour.
O eternal word, word of my God,
I want to spend my life in listening to you,
to become wholly teachable
that I may learn all from you.
Then, through all nights, all voids, all helplessness,
I want to gaze on you always and remain in your great light.

O my beloved star,
so fascinate me
that I may not withdraw from your radiance.
O consuming fire,
Spirit of love,
'come upon me,'

and create in my soul a kind of incarnation of the word:
that I may be another humanity for him
in which he can renew his whole mystery.

And you, O Father,
bend lovingly over your poor little creature,
'cover her with your shadow,'
seeing in her only
the 'beloved in whom you are well pleased.'

Bd Elizabeth of the Trinity

My God: without ceasing, I will tread the threshold of your house.
I will ask with boldness, that I may receive with confidence.
    For if, O Lord, the earth enriches manifold a single grain of
wheat, how then shall my prayers be enriched by your grace!
    Because of the voices of my children, their sighs and their
groans, open to me the door of your mercy: make glad their
voices, the mourning of their sackcloth.
    For a flock, O my Lord, in the field, if it has seen the
wolves, flees to the shepherd, and takes refuge under his staff,
and he drives them that would devour it.
    Your flock has seen the wolves, and lo! it cries loudly.
Behold: how terrified it is! Let your cross be a staff, to drive
out those who would swallow it up!
    Accept the cry of my little ones, who are altogether pure. It
was he, the infant of days, who could appease, O Lord, the
Ancient of Days.
    The day when the babe came down, in the midst of the
staff, the watchers descended and proclaimed peace: may that
peace be, in all my streets, for all my offspring.

Have mercy, O Lord, on my children! In my children, call
to mind your childhood, you who were a child! Let those who
are like your childhood be saved by your grace!

St Ephrem the Syrian

May my purpose not be judged
    by you, O knower of all things;
may my search not be held blameworthy
    by you, concealed from all;
for I have not made bold to speak
    of your generation, hidden from all;
in silence
    I have bounded the word.
Yet because I have honoured your birth,
    allow me to dwell in your Paradise.
From all who love you
    be praise to your hiddenness!

St Ephrem the Syrian

Have pity on me,
    O Lord of Paradise,
and if it is not possible for me
    to enter your Paradise,
grant that I may graze
    outside, by its enclosure;
within, let there be spread
    the table for the 'diligent,'
but may the fruits within its enclosure
    drop outside like the 'crumbs'

for sinners, so that, through your grace,
    they may live!

St Ephrem the Syrian

Grant, Lord, that I and those dear to me
    may together there
find the very last remnants
    of your gift!
Just the sight of your dear one
    is a fountain of delight;
whoever is worthy
    to be ravished thereby
will despise ordinary food;
    all who look upon you
will be sustained by your beauty.
    Praises be to your splendour!

St Ephrem the Syrian

Beloved Jesus, how great is your goodness, how creative is your love! O, if I could love you as much as I want to love you, and as much as I should! As another sign of your love, let me repeat to you my lovely refrain: 'I love you, Jesus, I love you so much, so very much. Enlarge my heart so that I can love you more and more.'

I want to be consumed for love of you, loving Jesus, consumed before you like a candle flame! O Jesus, Jesus, Jesus, I trust in you, do not leave me! Your love is an infinite ocean of light and grace.

My Jesus, you overcome me with the tenderness of your

unspeakable goodness. Your words are like sharp and penetrating arrows piercing my heart, the target of your flaming love!

Yes, Jesus, burn within me all that is unworthy of you. Strip me of everything not pleasing to you! In this land of exile, I want to love you with a love that is total and pure.

St Frances Cabrini

I love you, Jesus, but my heart is not satisfied, I am consumed by my thirst to love you!

I long to love you much more, immense goodness, enlarge my heart, fill it with your holy love!

Enlarge my heart so that I may be satisfied, my thirst will be quenched, loving you, with you, for you!

I drink from the fount of water which comes from you….I long for you!

St Frances Cabrini

My Jesus, grant me the grace to love you with all my heart, to serve you with great fidelity now so that I may be as a grain of sand in the monument to your glory for all eternity.

I abandon myself wholly to your good pleasure, do with me what you will. I am all yours—all yours! There is nothing good for me outside of you. I love creatures because they are yours; I want to love them always for your sake, to please you, to glorify you, and console your divine heart.

St Frances Cabrini

Let your voice sound within me, that I may understand what you want of me, that I may always find you to love you, love you to possess you, possess you to enjoy you!

Jesus, you want me to seek you with all my being, to find you, know, love, and glorify you, and to strive with all the strength you grant me, to have you served and honoured by all.

Yes, infinite goodness, through your mercy, you have made me a missionary of your divine heart, and I must, I will act as a missionary, relying on your help which is never lacking.

Let your voice sound within me, and I shall go even to the farthest end of the earth, to do all that you ask, because the sound of your voice performs wonders.

In your name, Jesus, and enclosed within your heart, I can do anything!

St Frances Cabrini

Agonizing heart of my Jesus, help me through the abandonment you experienced in the garden of Gethsemane, the horror you experienced seeing yourself covered by all my sins, your bloody sweat. Help me, I beseech you, give me courage to overcome all obstacles that make me less dear to you....Yes, yes, lovable Jesus, grant that I may keep you company here in the Garden of Olives in place of the disciples who sleep!

St Frances Cabrini

Enlarge my heart, beloved of my soul, and render me a little
more capable, for I cannot withstand your love any more.
Ocean of infinite love, I want to love you; but the more I love
you, the less I love, because I want to love you all the more. I
can't go on any more; enlarge…spread wide my heart.

St Frances Cabrini

My Lord, your mercy inspires me to suffer for your love and to
imitate your life which was one continual martyrdom of
suffering. Let me feel the desire to humble myself for love of
you. Show me how to do this, since in many circumstances I
almost don't feel the courage to follow your holy inspirations.

St Frances Cabrini

Give me your grace, most loving Jesus, and I will run after you
to the finish line, forever. Help me, Jesus, because I want to do
this with burning fervour, speedily.

St Frances Cabrini

O yes, my Lord, Jesus, I hear your call. You call me, Lord; here
I am. I hear your call. I thirst, my adorable Jesus; I am very
thirsty, almost to the point of collapse, innerly empty and
burned up. Take me to you and give me to drink from your
saving wells. Yes, please, Lord, plunge me into your heavenly
waters. Drown me in them; drown my passions, my pride, and
all my vices and faults, that whatever in me comes from myself
may die and the old creature be no more, and that there be
nothing else in me than you.

Ven. Francis Libermann

O my Lord Jesus! Teach me to be generous; teach me to serve you as you deserve; to give and not to count the cost; to fight and not to heed the wounds; to toil and not to ask for rest; to labour, seeking no reward, save that of knowing that I do your will. Amen.

St Francis Xavier

O God of all the nations of the earth: Remember the multitudes who have been created in your image, and who yet do not know the fullness of your truth and love in the death of your Son, Jesus Christ. Grant that by the prayers and labours of your Church they may be delivered from all superstition and unbelief, and brought to worship you through him whom you have sent to be the resurrection and the life of all mankind, your Son our saviour Jesus Christ. Amen.

St Francis Xavier

O Eternal Love: My soul desires and chooses you eternally. Ah, come, Holy Spirit: Inflame our hearts with your love! To love or to die, to die and to love: to die to all other love in order to live to Jesus' love, that we may not die eternally, but that, living in your eternal love, O saviour of our souls, we may eternally sing: Blessed be Jesus, who lives and reigns forever! Amen.

St Francis de Sales

May your heart always dwell in our hearts!
May your blood always flow in the veins of our souls!

O sun of our hearts!
You give life to all things by the rays of your goodness:

I will not go until your heart has strengthened me, O Lord Jesus!

O may the heart of Jesus be the king of mine!
Blessed be God! Amen.

St Francis de Sales

I beseech you, O Lord, that the fiery and sweet strength of
your love may absorb my soul from all things that are under
heaven, that I may die for love of your love as you deigned to
die for love of my love.

St Francis of Assisi

Almighty, eternal, just, and merciful God, give to us wretches
to do for you what we know you to will, and to will always
that which is pleasing to you; so that inwardly purified,
inwardly illumined and kindled by the flame of the Holy
Spirit, we may be able to follow in the footsteps of your Son,
our Lord Jesus Christ, and by your grace alone come to you
the Most High, who in perfect Trinity and simple unity lives
and reigns and glories, God Almighty forever and ever. Amen.

St Francis of Assisi

We beseech thee, O God, the God of truth
That what we know not of things we ought to know thou wilt
teach us.

That what we know of truth thou wilt keep us therein.
That what we are mistaken in, as men must be, thou wilt correct.
That at whatsoever truths we stumble, thou wilt yet establish us.
And from all things that are false and from all knowledge that
would be hurtful, thou wilt evermore deliver us,
Through Jesus Christ our Lord. Amen.

St Fulgentius

My Jesus, I paid you ever so many little visits: do not abandon
me now, O Jesus, my Love!

St Gabriel Possenti

May the most holy, adorable, and amiable will of God be ever
done, by all creatures.

St Gabriel Possenti

Make haste, Jesus; O, do you not see how this heart longs for
you? O, do you not see how it languishes? Does it not pain
you, O God, to see it thus languish in desire? Come! come,
Jesus, make haste, come near, let me hear your voice. O God,
when shall my whole being be satiated with your divine light,
O when? Jesus, food of strong souls, strengthen, purify me,
make me divine, great God, Jesus, help me. God begotten of
God, come to my aid, I thirst for you, Jesus. Do you not see
how I suffer every morning until I feed on you? Grant, at least,
that thus nourished I may remain satisfied.

St Gemma Galgani

O Jesus, if it is pleasing to you, give me a little respite! I feel myself growing faint. A little respite, Jesus!

St Gemma Galgani

Lord, grant me grace to sever all the ties that bind me to this earth, to renounce all worldly trifles, to free myself from all kinds of worldly desires, appetites, pursuits, and plans so that I may boldly say: I no longer fear anyone on earth, I only fear you, my Lord, my God and Creator; I fear only that I may please you less than I am able, that I may do less for your glory than my powers, aided by your grace, can perform.

Bd George Matulaitis

O gift surpassing all gifts, to be satisfied with the sweetness of the Divinity, and to be superabundantly inebriated with divine charity in the cellar where it is reserved; so that our feet are no longer free to roam to any place where its divine fragrance is not perceived: unless, indeed, they are led forth by charity, when they pour out on others the wealth of divine faithfulness, and enable them to partake of their surpassing sweetness.

I hope, my Lord and my God, that you, in your most benign love, will grant me this grace, which by your almighty power you can impart to all your elect. It is true your inscrutable wisdom alone knows how you can do this, notwithstanding my unworthiness. But I honour and I glorify your wise and merciful almightiness; I glorify and magnify your almighty and all-merciful wisdom; I praise and adore your wise and omnipotent mercy; I bless and thank your

omnipotent and wise kindness, O my God, because you have
bestowed on me graces so far beyond my deserts,
notwithstanding all the obstacles I opposed to your bounty.

St Gertrude of Helfta

O you who are long suffering, who are of great mercy and
great truth: Take at our hands our prayers and supplications;
place our cry, repentance, and our confession upon your
unblemished altar in heaven! May we be worthy to hear your
holy gospel, to keep your commandments, your holy precepts,
to yield from them fruit, a hundredfold, seventyfold, and
fortyfold, through Jesus Christ our Lord.

St Gregory Nazianzen

Lord and Creator of all, especially of your creature man, you
are the God and Father and ruler of all your children; you are
the Lord of life and death, the guardian and benefactor of our
souls.

You fashion and transform all things in their due course
through your creative word, as you know to be the best in
your great wisdom and providence. Receive those who have
gone ahead of us in our journey from this life.

Receive us, too, at the proper time when you have guided
us in our earthly life as long as you see it is good. May we set
out eagerly for that everlasting and blessed life which is in
Jesus Christ, our Lord. To him be glory for ever and ever.
Amen.

St Gregory Nazianzen

I entreat you, O Lord, Holy Father, Everlasting God:
Command the way of your truth and of the knowledge of you
to be shown to your servants who wander in doubt and
uncertainty amid the darkness of this world; that the eyes of
their souls may be opened, and that they may acknowledge
you, the one God, the Father in the Son, and the Son in the
Father, with the Holy Spirit, and enjoy the fruit of this
confession, both here and in the life to come: through Jesus
Christ our Lord, who lives and reigns with God the Father, in
the unity of the Holy Spirit, God, now and eternally: Amen.

St Gregory the Great

O Lord, mingle our humanity with your divinity, your
greatness with our humility, and our humility with your
greatness, that we may offer acceptably this offering, which
you made for the redemption of humankind.

St Gregory the Great

Ah, boundless Good, you who fill the kingdoms of heaven and
earth, incline graciously toward me and despise not your poor
creature! Lord, if I am not worthy of you, at least I am in need
of you. Ah, gentle Lord, are you not the one who with a single
word created heaven and earth? Lord, with a single word you
can heal my sick soul. Alas, gentle Lord, deal with me
according to your infinite mercy, not according to my
deserving. You are truly the innocent Paschal Lamb that is
offered today for the sins of all men.

Sweet, savoury Bread of Heaven, having all delightful
flavour according to the desire of every heart, grant that the

dry mouth of my soul may find delight in you today. Feed me and give me to drink. Strengthen and adorn me, and unite yourself intimately with me. Eternal Wisdom, enter so powerfully into my soul that you will drive out all my foes, melt away all my faults, and forgive all my sins. Enlighten my understanding with the light of your true faith; inflame my will with your delightful love; illumine my memory with your gladsome presence; and give virtue and perfection to all my faculties. Guard me at the moment of death, so that I may enjoy you face to face in everlasting bliss. Amen.

Bd Henry Suso

O you most beautiful, most brilliant Eternal Wisdom, my soul has yearned for you during the night. Now in this early morning hour, my heart and soul have awakened to you, my love. I beg you, my gracious Lord, that your coveted presence will drive all evil far from my body and soul, pour precious graces into every dark nook of my being, and inflame my cold heart with the fire of divine love. Ah, sweetest Jesus Christ, turn your gracious countenance kindly toward me, because this morning my soul turns to you with all its faculties. I tenderly greet you from the deepest depth of my heart and desire that the thousand times a thousand angels who serve you would today greet you for me, and that the ten thousand times a hundred thousand heavenly spirits who dwell with you would praise you worthily. May the fair loveliness of all creatures praise you today in union with me, and gratefully bless your sacred name, our comforting shield, now and throughout the ageless eternity. Amen.

Bd Henry Suso

Ah, boundless goodness, how tenderly you now prove your love for me. When I did not exist, you created me; when I abandoned you, you refused to leave me; when I tried to run away from you, you held me captive in love's chains. Eternal wisdom, my heart now desires to burst open, to be shattered into a thousand pieces, to embrace you with constant love, and to consume all my days in perfect praise of you....

Alas, dear, lovable Wisdom, now that I have found the fulfillment of my soul's desires in you, despise not your poor creature but consider how insensible my heart is toward everything earthly, in joy and in sorrow. Lord, do you want my heart to repress its holy love-making? Permit, O Lord, permit my weary soul to whisper a few words with you, because my full heart can no longer keep its secret. There is no one in this wide world in whom my heart can confide except you, gentle, precious, beloved Lord and brother. Lord, you alone see and understand the nature of an affectionate heart....since I am obliged to love you alone, teach me to know you better so that I may love you in full measure.

Bd Henry Suso

Almighty and loving God, I believe that by reason of your immensity you are present everywhere. You are here, within me, and have seen my most hidden thoughts and affections of my soul.

I cannot hide myself from your divine presence.

I adore you, from the depth of my misery and nothingness.

I ask you pardon from all my sins, which I detest with all my strength.

I beg you the grace to profit by this brief time of prayer,
which I offer to your greater glory.

Eternal Father, teach me to pray, to know myself and you,
to love you always, and to make you known and loved. Amen.

St Henry de Osso

I trust in you, Lord.

I desire to forget myself and leave my own cares until I trust
you with all and nothing worries me.

Give me peace because in your mercy I put my hope.

St Henry de Osso

I believe in you, Lord,
    increase my faith.
I hope in you, Lord,
    increase my hope.
I love you, Lord,
    increase my love
until I love you as much as I can,
and if possible as much as you love me. Amen.

St Henry de Osso

O Lord: Keep us from vain strife of words: Grant to us a
constant profession of the truth!

Preserve us in the faith, true and undefiled, that we may
always hold fast to what we professed when we were baptized
to, and in the name of, Father, Son, and Holy Spirit—

That we may have you for our Father,

That we may abide in your Son,

And in the fellowship of the Holy Spirit:
Through the same Jesus Christ, our Lord. Amen.

St Hilary of Poitiers

Praise to you
Spirit of fire!
to you who sound the timbrel
and the lyre.

Your music sets our minds
ablaze! The strength of our souls
awaits your coming
in the tent of meeting.

There the mounting will
gives the soul its savour
and desire is its lantern.

Insight invokes you in a cry
full of sweetness, while reason
builds you temples as she labours
at her golden crafts.

But sword
in hand you stand poised
to prune shoots of the poisoned
apple—
scions of the darkest
murder—

when mist overshadows the will.
Adrift in desires the soul is spinning

everywhere. But the mind
is a bond
to bind will and desire.

When the heart yearns to look
the Evil One in the eye,
to stare down the jaws of
iniquity, swiftly
you burn it in consuming
fire. Such is your wish.

And when reason doing ill
falls from her place, you
restrain and constrain her as you will
in the flow of experience until
she obeys you.

And when the Evil One brandishes
his sword against you,
you break it in his own
heart. For so you did
to the first lost angel,
tumbling the tower of his
arrogance to hell.

And there you built a second
tower—traitors and sinners
its stones. In repentance
they confessed all their crafts.

So all beings that live by you
praise your outpouring
like a priceless salve upon [festering]

sores, upon fractured
limbs. You convert them
into priceless gems!

Now gather us all to yourself
and in your mercy guide us
into the paths of justice.

St Hildegard of Bingen

Take, Lord, all my freedom. Accept all my memory, intellect,
and will. All that I have or possess, you have given to me; all I
give back to you, and give up then to be governed by your
will. Grant me only the grace to love you, and I am sufficiently
rich so that I do not ask for anything else.

St Ignatius of Loyola

Teach us, good Lord, to serve you as you deserve; to give, and
not to count the cost; to fight, and not to heed the wounds; to
toil, and not to seek for rest; to labour, and not to ask for any
reward, save that of knowing that we do your will; through
Jesus Christ our Lord.

St Ignatius of Loyola

Lord Jesus Christ, your compassion caused you to suffer to
save the world. May the heavens open and the angels receive
my spirit, for I am suffering for you and your Church in this
place. I beseech you, merciful Lord, please take me to yourself
and strengthen the faith of your servants who remain.

St Irenaeus of Sirmium

O my Lord, I am in a dry land, all dried up and cracked by the violence of the north wind and the cold; but as you see, I ask for nothing more; you will send me both dew and warmth when it pleases you.

St Jane de Chantal

You know well what is happening, my dear Jesus. I have only you. Come to my aid.

Bd Jeanne Jugan

Lord our God, of boundless might, and incomprehensible glory, and measureless compassion, and ineffable love to man, look down, O Lord, according to your tender love, on us, and on this holy house, and show to us, and to them that pray with us, the riches of your mercies and compassions.

St John Chrysostom

Lord our God, save your people, and bless your inheritance; guard the fullness of your Church: hallow them that love the beauty of your house. Glorify them in recompense with your divine power: and forsake not them that put their trust in you.

St John Chrysostom

O Lord and lover of men, cause the pure light of your divine knowledge to shine forth in our hearts, and open the eyes of our understanding, that we may comprehend the precepts of your gospel. Plant in us also the fear of your blessed commandments, that we, trampling upon all carnal lusts, may seek a heavenly citizenship, both saying and doing always such things as shall well please you. For you are the illumination of our souls and bodies, Christ our God; and to you we ascribe all glory, honour, and worship, Father, Son, and Holy Spirit, now and ever, and to ages of ages.

St John Chrysostom

Lord our God, we pray you to receive this intense supplication from your servants, according to the multitude of your mercy, and send down your compassion upon us, and upon all your people, who are expecting the rich mercy that is from you.

St John Chrysostom

Remember, Lord, the city in which we dwell, and every city and region, and the faithful that inhabit it. Remember, Lord, those that voyage, and travel, that are sick, that are labouring, that are in prison, and their safety. Remember, Lord, those that bear fruit, and do good deeds in your holy churches, and that remember the poor. And send forth on us all the riches of your compassion, and grant us with one mouth and one heart to glorify and celebrate your glorious and majestic name, Father, Son, and Holy Spirit, now and ever, and to ages of ages. And the mercies of the great God and our saviour Jesus Christ shall be with all of us.

St John Chrysostom

Lord, who blesses those that bless you, and sanctifies those that put their trust in you, save your people, and bless your inheritance: guard with care the fullness of your Church: hallow those that love the beauty of your house. Glorify them in return by your divine might, and forsake not those that put their trust in you; give your peace to your world, to your churches…and to all your people; because every good gift and every perfect gift is from above, and comes down from you, the Father of lights….

St John Chrysostom

O Christ our God, who are yourself the fullness of the Law and of the Prophets, who accomplished all the dispensation of your Father, fill our hearts with joy and gladness always, now and ever, and to ages of ages. Amen.

St John Chrysostom

Loving God, I ask for the grace of light to know all the good I should do and the evil I should avoid. I ask for the grace of strength so as to overcome temptations and to face courageously the difficulty and repugnance I find in doing good.

Bd John Martin Moye

Holy, wise, generous, and loving providence! I thank you for
the tender care you have taken of me up to this moment. I
humbly and earnestly entreat you to continue the same for
me. Direct all that I do, guide me in your ways, govern me at
every moment of my life. Dispose of me and of all that belongs
to me as you please (and bring me into the fullness of being
that you have destined for me from all eternity) for your
greater glory and my salvation. Amen.

Bd John Martin Moye

My Jesus, how good it is to love you! Let me be like your
disciples on Mount Tabor, seeing nothing else but you, my
saviour. Let us be as two friends, neither of whom can ever
bear to offend the other. Amen.

St John Vianney

Jesus, my Lord and saviour, what can I give you in return for
all the favours you have first conferred on me? I will take from
your hand the cup of your sufferings and call on your name....
    My beloved Jesus, here and now I offer my body and blood
and life. May I die only for you, if you will grant me this grace,
since you willingly died for me. Let me so live that you may
grant me the gift of such a happy death. In this way, my God
and saviour, I will take from your hand the cup of your
sufferings and call on your name: Jesus, Jesus, Jesus!

St John de Brébeuf

Awake us, O Lord, and enlighten us, that we may know and love the good things that you have set always before us, and we shall know that you are moved to do us good, and have remembered us.

St John of the Cross

This life that I am living
Is a lifeless life.
And so a death continuing,
Until I come to live with you.
O God, hear my cry!
This life of mine I will it not;
I die because I am not dead.

St John of the Cross

O Lord, my bridegroom, who gave me yourself partially before, give me yourself wholly now. You who did show glimpses of yourself before, show yourself clearly now. You who did communicate yourself hitherto by the instrumentality of messengers—it was as if you mocked me—give yourself by yourself now. Sometimes when you visited me you gave me the pearl of your possession, and, when I began to examine it, lo, it was gone, for you had hidden it yourself: it was like a mockery. Give me then yourself in truth, your whole self, that I may have you wholly to myself wholly, and send me no messengers again.

St John of the Cross

O faith of Christ my bridegroom! O that you would manifest clearly those truths concerning the beloved, secretly and obscurely infused—for faith is, as theologians say, an obscure habit—so that your informal and obscure communications may be in a moment clear; O that you would withdraw yourself formally and completely from these truths—for faith is a veil over the truths of God—and reveal them perfectly in glory.

St John of the Cross

Hold dominion over my heart, O Lord: keep it as your inheritance. Make your dwelling in me, along with the Father and the Holy Spirit. Widen in me the cords of your tabernacle, even the operations of your most Holy Spirit. For you are my God, and I will praise you, together with the eternal Father, and your life-giving Spirit, now, henceforth, and forever. Amen.

St John of Damascus

O great, most sacred passover of Christ! O wisdom, power, word of God, grant that we may see your presence in your kingdom, in that day that has no evening! Amen.

St John of Damascus

I understand the call of your heart, good Master, and I am indeed desirous of responding to it. I offer myself entirely to you, for love of you. I wish to be completely dependent on you, to do everything for you and with you. Accept my oblation, bless it, nourish it by your grace, that it may be generous and persevering.

Ven. Leo John Dehon

My God, by the revelation of the august mystery of your Trinity you have illumined our faith with the most vivid splendours; in confessing this mystery you have given us the most solid basis for our hope. Grant that we may also find there the most secure bond and stirring example of charity.

All powerful Father, you have formed our hearts and you draw them to what pleases you; Son, equal to your Father, but made flesh for us, you have gathered us under the same law of love; Holy Spirit, you are the substantial love of the Father and the Son and through you this charity is poured out in our hearts; Holy Trinity, it is from your side that all of us have come forth and it is to your side that all of us want to be drawn back! Unite us on earth in faith, hope, and charity, as we are going to be united in that blessed eternity where your grace is leading us. Amen.

Ven. Leo John Dehon

My Jesus, before you and your heavenly Father, in the presence of Mary Immaculate, my mother, and of St Joseph, my protector, I vow out of pure love to devote myself to your sacred heart....I accept in advance all the trials and sacrifices that it pleases you to ask of me. I vow to make pure love for Jesus and his sacred heart the intention of my every act. I ask you to touch my heart and fire it with your love, so that I may have not only the intention and desire of loving you, but also through the work of your grace, the happiness of having all the affections of my heart centred on you alone.

Ven. Leo John Dehon

You have given me the grace to begin to love you, my good Master. Give me the grace to persevere in your love, cost what it may. It is in a spirit of love that I wish to offer you constantly my daily actions, works, and sufferings.

Ven. Leo John Dehon

Grant to us, O Lord, not to mind earthly things, but rather to love heavenly things, that while all things around us pass away, we even now may hold fast those things that abide forever.

St Leo the Great

O Lord: Give to your people, we pray, the Spirit of truth and of peace, that they may know you with all their minds; and that following with all their hearts after those things that are pleasing to you, they may ever possess the gifts of your bountiful goodness.

St Leo the Great

Protect, O Lord, those who cry to you for help. Uphold us in our weakness, and cleanse us from our earthliness: and while we walk in this dying life amidst the shadows of death, enliven us with your light. In your mercy, deliver us from all evil, so that we may come to the perfection of all good at last.

St Leo the Great

Come, O divine food, to nourish my soul! Come, O flames of love: enkindle me! Come, O heavenly shepherd, to guide me! Come, O Father! O my bridegroom! O my life! Come, the sole object of my desires! Come, O light of souls! O refreshment of hearts! O comforter of the afflicted!

Come: for you have all nations waited: for you have the patriarchs sighed. Come: desire of the everlasting hills, joy of the angels, rapturous delight of heaven!

Bliss of the saints! Come, my Paradise: for you do I long, for you do I sigh. Come: you have wounded me with your love. Come, tarry no longer: I am being consumed with desire. How can I live any longer without you? Have mercy on me, then, O my Jesus! Come!

St Leonard

My God, just as I wish to love nothing more than you, so I wish to live only for you. I offer you all my thoughts, all my words, all my actions, and all my sufferings this day; please bestow your holy blessing upon them. Amen.

St Louis Marie Grignion de Montfort

My Jesus, I long ardently
For you to come to me this day;
Without you life is misery.
Come to me soon, I pray.

Without the fervour that you bring,
O Love, I languish night and day;
And do you not desire my love?
Inflame my heart, I pray.

Good Shepherd, bear your lost sheep home
Within your arms, whene'er I stray;
From ravening wolves that round me roam
Oh, keep me safe, I pray.

O Bread of Life, for you I sigh,
Give me yourself without delay;
For otherwise my soul must die.
Give me to eat, I pray.

O fount of living waters clear,
How long and weary is the way;
Refresh my soul which thirsts for you.
Give me to drink, I pray.

O loving Lord, my soul is chilled
By icy winds that round me play;
O fire of love, let me be filled
With warmth from you, I pray.

Like the blind man who cried to you:
Have mercy on me, Lord, I say,
O Mary's son, that I may see;
Increase my faith, I pray.

Lord, I am sick beyond all cure,
But with a word you can display
Your power; without you death is sure.
O heal me, Lord, I pray.

My Lord, I knock upon your door;
Your favours I can ne'er repay.
Yet in my want I beg for more.
Fulfill my needs, I pray.

I am not worthy, Lord, that you
Should come into my house today
As heavenly food; say but the word
And heal my soul, I pray.

Lord, you alone are my true friend,
My treasure which can ne'er decay;
All earthly joys do you transcend.
Do visit me this day.

St Louis Marie Grignion de Montfort

May you be pleased, O my God, to confirm these resolutions
and receive them with an odour of sweetness. And since you
were pleased to inspire me to make them, give me the grace to
carry them out, O my God....You are my God and my all; I
adore and recognize you as such. One only true God in three
persons, now, and for all eternity.

St Louise de Marillac

May I have no will of my own, O Lord, but let yours reign
alone in me! Give me this grace by your love for me, and by
the intercession of your blessed Mother—whose love for that
most tender will was so perfect. I ask this of you with all my
heart, begging of your goodness to pay no regard to the
contrary dispositions you see in me, desiring that the strength
of your love should overpower with its sweet violence the
resistance of all that is in me to its fulfillment. Thus I will go to
this new habitation with the design of honouring the divine
providence who leads me there, and try to put myself in the
disposition to accomplish what this same providence permits

me to find there to do. I will by this change of abode honour
that of Jesus and the blessed Virgin from Bethlehem to Egypt,
and to so many other places, not wishing any more than they
did to have any lasting abode on earth.

St Louise de Marillac

I implore the goodness of God to continue to bestow his lights
and his guidance upon his work, and to destroy all obstacles
to it, and to reveal his will on the subject of those he desires to
see associated with it.

St Louise de Marillac

I earnestly implore the sacred heart of Jesus, by our Lady of
the seven sorrows, to restore to me by a gift of the mercy of
Jesus Christ, the method of prayer I once had, and which I
have lost by long unfaithfulness.

St Madeleine Sophie Barat

Jesus, my sweetest life, hear this my earnest entreaty. Grant
that I may die completely to myself that you alone may live in
me. Grant that the silence within me may be like that of the
dead, that you alone may speak to my heart. May I do
nothing, that you may work in me all that you will.

St Madeleine Sophie Barat

Hail, heart of my Jesus: save me!
Hail, heart of my creator: perfect me!
Hail, heart of my saviour: deliver me!
Hail, heart of my judge: pardon me!

Hail, heart of my Father: govern me!
Hail, heart of my Master: teach me!
Hail, heart of my King: crown me!
Hail, heart of my benefactor: enrich me!
Hail, heart of my pastor: guard me!
Hail, heart of my brother: stay with me!
Hail, heart of my incomparable goodness: have mercy on me!
Hail, most loving heart: inflame me. Amen.

St Margaret Mary Alacoque

I offer myself to you, O heart of my Jesus, with the intention
that all my life, all my sufferings, all my actions, all my being
are to be employed in loving you, adoring you, glorifying you.
I wish that my heart would be consumed and reduced to ashes
through the vehemence of its love for you! Why am I not all
heart to love you, and all spirit to adore you? I beseech you
that henceforth I may love only you, and all things in you and
for you!

St Margaret Mary Alacoque

God, Holy Spirit, grant me the grace daily and hourly to grow
in love for you. Help me to grow ever more insignificant
through humility but ever greater in holy love. Grant me the
grace to always walk in the presence of God, not give way to
sadness when neglected or humiliated, but rather thank God
with a sincere love of sacrifice. Amen.

Bd Maria Helena Stollenwerk

O most loving heart of Jesus, I commend to you this night my
heart and soul that they may rest peacefully in you. Since I
cannot praise you while I sleep, may my guardian angel
replace me that all my heart's beats may be so many acts of
praise and thanksgiving offered to your loving heart and that
of the eternal Father. Amen.

St Maria Soledad Torres Acosta

My God, if you delay the opening of the doors of your home
to me, it is because you are asking something else of me; show
me your will.

St Maria Soledad Torres Acosta

Heart of Jesus, protect me!

St Maria Soledad Torres Acosta

My enraptured spirit contemplates all your works.
    Who can speak of you, O God so great!
    O omnipotent one, (it is) my ravished soul!
A nothing, a bit of dust says to you: Come to me.
    Who can say that an omnipotent one takes notice!
One glance! You who look at me, come to me.
    You alone, my God, my all.
I see you, goodness supreme: your glance is maternal.
Come quickly, O sun of justice, arise!
My soul is consumed, I languish while waiting,
    Come quickly!

Bd Mariam Baouardy

O blessed cross! come to my embrace. Yet more, O Lord; give me yet more to bear.

St Marie-Madeleine Postel

O divine Father, please give me this faith that will unite me to your Son and make me one body with him....Please give me those daily graces necessary to be fruitful in virtue and good works.

Bd Marie of the Incarnation

My Lord, you ask me to suffer, and so my poor soul desires to do that. But, O Jesus, I want to suffer only with you, for love of you; to suffer in silence and solitude so that only you would know that I suffer, only you would hear the moaning of my heart and see my tears. Ah, Lord, teach me to suffer in this way. Teach me to suffer without seeking any compassion or sympathy from creatures, to suffer without even looking forward to the eternal joys of heaven. Teach me to suffer not because suffering is the source of merit and glory, but because it leads us to union with you and makes our hearts like unto yours.

Teach me to suffer with such a love for your divine will that I would not choose my own crosses but humbly accept those that you yourself give; that I would not even for a moment desire any relief; and that I would not even know how to long for heaven unless you alone, O Lord, fill my heart with this yearning. Teach me to so love suffering as you loved the cross; teach me to so desire suffering as you desired it. Teach me to suffer with such silence, purity, and love as your most pure

Mother suffered when you left her orphaned on this earth. As you permitted her, so permit me to die from this sorrow, longing, and love, and then do with me as you please.

Grant only that I may love you forever and, if such be your will, that I may suffer for you forever, provided only that I live in your love, be yours, and praise your most blessed will for all eternity.

Bd Mary Angela Truszkowska

Give me so strong a voice, O my Lord, that while I call you Lord, I may be heard from the East to the West, and throughout all the parts of the world, even to hell itself, that you may be known and reverenced as the true love. O love, O love, which only penetrates and transcends, which breaks and binds, which rules and governs all things! You are heaven and earth, fire and air, blood and water; you are God and man. And who shall ever be able either to express or to think of your greatness, since you are infinite and eternal!

St Mary Magdalene dei Pazzi

Lord, since you have taken from all that I had of you, yet of your grace leave the gift that every dog has by nature: that of being true to you in my distress, when I am deprived of all consolation. This I desire more fervently than your heavenly kingdom!

St Mechtilde

Blessed Father, eternal, binding all creation together by your strength, taking the heavens for your abode: May we also pass beyond the gates of life, welcomed by you, O Father, and your Son.

St Methodius of Olympus

My Lord and my God, take from me everything that distances me from you.

My Lord and my God, give me everything that brings me closer to you.

My Lord and my God, detach me from myself to give my all to you.

St Nicholas of Flüe

Son of the Highest, deign to cast
On us a pitying eye,
You who repentant Magdalen
Called to endless joy.

O Jesus, balm of every wound!
The sinners' only stay!
Wash in Magdalen's pure tears
Our guilty spots away.

St Odo of Cluny

I

I bind myself today,
To a strong power, an invocation of the Trinity,
I believe in a threeness with confession of a oneness in the creator of judgment.

II

I bind myself today,
    To the power of the birth of Christ, with his baptism,
    To the power of the crucifixion, with his burial,
    To the power of his resurrection, with his ascension,
    To the power of his coming to the judgment of doom.

III

I bind myself today,
    To the power of the ranks of cherubim,
    In the obedience of angels,
    In the service of archangels,
    In the hope of resurrection unto reward,
    In the prayers of patriarchs,
    In the predictions of prophets,
    In the preachings of apostles,
    In the faiths of confessors,
    In the purity of holy virgins,
    In the acts of righteous men.

IV

I bind myself today,
    To the power of heaven,
    The light of sun,
    The brightness of moon,
    The splendour of fire,
    The speed of lightning,
    The swiftness of wind,
    The depth of the sea,
    The stability of earth,
    The firmness of rocks

V

I bind myself today,
> To the power of God to guide me,
> The might of God to uphold me,
> The wisdom of God to teach me,
> The eye of God to watch over me,
> The ear of God to hear me,
> The word of God to speak for me,
> The hand of God to protect me,
> The way of God to lie before me,
> The shield of God to shelter me,
> The host of God to defend me,
>> Against the snares of demons,
>> Against the temptations of vices,
>> Against [the lusts] of nature,
>> Against every man who meditates injury to me,
>>> Whether far or near,
>>> Alone and in a multitude.

VI

I summon today around me all these powers,
> Against every hostile merciless power directed against my body and my soul,
> Against the incantations of false prophets,
> Against the black laws of heathenism,
> Against the false laws of heretics,
> Against the deceit of idolatry,
> Against the spells of smiths, and druids,
> Against all knowledge that has defiled man's body and soul.

VII

Christ protect me today,
    Against poison, against burning,
    Against drowning, against wound,
    That I may receive a multitude of rewards.

VIII

Christ with me, Christ before me,
Christ behind me, Christ within me,
Christ beneath me, Christ above me,
Christ at my right, Christ at my left,
Christ in breadth, Christ in length, Christ in height.

IX

Christ in the heart of every man who thinks of me,
Christ in the mouth of every man who speaks to me,
Christ in the eye of every man that sees me,
Christ in the ear of every man that hears me.

X

I bind myself today,
    To a strong power, an invocation of the Trinity,
    I believe in a threeness with confession of a oneness in the
creator of judgment.

XI

Salvation is the Lord's,
Salvation is the Lord's,
Salvation is Christ's,
Let your salvation, O Lord, be ever with us.

St Patrick

Lord, I know that what I have tried to say, what you have enabled me to see and feel to some degree, is truly ineffable, unfathomable….But grant, Lord, that what I cannot understand intellectually nor express in writing, I may taste and enjoy by experience….Grant that I may be united to you in a way that the mind cannot grasp nor the pen express, that I may be so totally absorbed in you that I may love you and rejoice in you. I do not ask that your joy may enter my being, but rather that I, like the faithful servant, may enter into that joy, that I may wholly lose myself, be annihilated to myself, and taste your love in a manner beyond all telling or understanding.

Bd Paul Giustiniani

Lord, help me be a soul of prayer; help me that all my works swim in prayer.

Bd Pauline von Mallinckrodt

Lord, I want so much to be like clay in your hands. Do with me as you wish, if only you do not withdraw your hand from me. Lead me as you wish over mountains and valleys, through deserts and swamps, over cliffs and boulders—it is all the same to me. As long as you lead me, I know that I am advancing toward my goal.

Bd Pauline von Mallinckrodt

O Lord, in all occurrences, in all business affairs, even the most unpleasant, help me strive for that calmness and equanimity that are so difficult for impulsive characters, but so blessed and meritorious, assuring us of God's blessing.

Bd Pauline von Mallinckrodt

Give me love, O Jesus, a most ardent love of neighbour. If I have you and it, then I am rich enough. O, give me this love. Give me the hearts of all you wish to entrust to me.

Bd Pauline von Mallinckrodt

O dearest Lord, teach me complete detachment from all things, all opinions, all creatures, so that I may find you, find you more perfectly and rest in you, labour in you, be completely united with you in the innermost depths of my will.

Bd Pauline von Mallinckrodt

Jesus, send me your Holy Spirit and I will overcome every obstacle successfully. You are strong in the weak, and this strength defies the world with all its vanities and dangers, resists hell, defies the weakness and frailty of my own heart. Lord Jesus, give me your Holy Spirit, that I may love and praise you, glorify you, and be your handmaid with whom you deal according to your will. Amen.

Bd Pauline von Mallinckrodt

O fountainhead of love, grant me a true motherly heart for all. Let me show the warmest love not only to those closest to me, but to all, that they may experience its benefits.

Bd Pauline von Mallinckrodt

Lord, teach me discernment of spirits. Teach me to be discerning not only in regard to myself but also in regard to others; this latter is so very necessary for me. Lord, you are faithful; help me! Lead me by the hand through all the circumstances of life. I follow you; arrange all for me! You be my light!

Bd Pauline von Mallinckrodt

O God, impress your image on me, form it in me! If it was worth your while to come down from heaven and to live here for thirty-three years to give me an example with such extravagance of love and labour—should it then be too much for me to study it? My Lord, let it be my meditation day and night. Impress it deeply and ever more deeply on my heart. Amen.

Bd Pauline von Mallinckrodt

Grant me solid, manifest virtues, so that I may not only be like a sturdy lighthouse, but also like a ship calmly advancing in the midst of storms. The pilot constantly looks at the compass or the Pole Star and guides his ship accordingly. Be my compass, O Jesus, be my star! If the Lord wills he can very quickly command the storms and we can land as though there had been no storm, as though we had been constantly sailing forward calmly. Lord, teach me the great art always to advance serenely, continually to grow in the interior life, happen what may. I do not want to steer once to the right and then to the left, but rather always straight ahead toward you, my compass, my star.

Bd Pauline von Mallinckrodt

Grant, O Jesus, that your image be formed in me, that I live only from you and in you and with you and through you— you the vine and I the branch. Help me that all my views and opinions so resemble yours that others, as it were, see Christ in me.

Bd Pauline von Mallinckrodt

From your hands, O Lord, I will accept everything you send me. Help me to become a saint. That is my one concern.

Bd Pauline von Mallinckrodt

The Lord grant to me here that both in me and for me he be a consuming fire. May my heart burn for me with this fire to life everlasting, so that my soul should not burn with it to eternal punishment.

St Paulinus of Nola

O God, the refuge of the poor, the strength of those who toil, and the comforter of all who sorrow, we commend to your mercy the unfortunate and the needy in whatever land they may be.

You alone know the number and extent of their sufferings and trials. Look down, Father of mercies, at those unhappy families suffering from war and slaughter, from hunger and illness and other severe troubles.

Spare them, O Lord, for it is truly a time of mercy. Amen.

St Peter Canisius

Hear me, O Lord, my soul's delight, joy of my heart, not because of my merits, but because of your boundless goodness. Teach me, enlighten me, direct me; help me in all things and by all things, that I may never say or do anything but what I know to be pleasing in your sight. Guide me, O God, my love, my light, and my life!

St Peter of Alcantara

O God of my heart! why do you not bestow your gifts on your poor servant who is in need and implores your help? You fill heaven and earth with blessings: why do you leave my heart empty? You, who clothe and adorn the lilies and flowers of the field, feed the birds of the air, and protect the tiniest of living creatures: why do you forget me, seeing that I desire to forget all through love of you?

St Peter of Alcantara

O sublime, most kind, and merciful Trinity! Father, Son, and Holy Spirit, one and only true God: teach, guide, and help me in all.

Almighty Father: by the might of your immense power, I beseech you, keep my memory fixed on you alone, and fill me with holy, devout thoughts.

O God the Son, eternal wisdom: enlighten my feeble intellect; steep it in the understanding of highest truths, and also of my poverty-stricken state.

Holy Spirit, love of the Father for the Son: make my will conformable to your most holy will, and inflame it with so powerful a fire of love for you that no waters arising from the storm of evil provocations may ever quench it.

St Peter of Alcantara

O only-begotten Jesus Christ, word of the eternal Father: Hear me invoke your clemency!

Speak peace, I beseech you, to the tempest that shakes your Church, and with the effusion of the blood of one who is your servant, end the persecution of your people, Lord. Amen.

St Peter of Alexandria

Lord, take care of me, lest I betray you and do you all the evil in the world if you do not help me.

St Philip Neri

Do with me, O Lord, as you will and know to be best.

St Philip Neri

Lord, I pray you, let me rest a little.

St Philip Neri

I would gladly do good, my Jesus, but I do not know how.
I would gladly seek you, my Jesus, but I do not know the way.
I would gladly serve you, my Jesus, but I do not know how.
I wish to love you, my Jesus, but I know not how.

I seek you and cannot find you; come to me, my Jesus.
I cannot love you unless you help me, my Jesus.
Unless you help me, O my Jesus, I know not what to do.
Jesus, be a Jesus to me.

St Philip Neri

I

O my Lord Jesus Christ crucified, Son of the most blessed
Virgin Mary, open your ears, and listen to me as you listened
to the eternal Father on Mount Tabor. *Credo.*

II

O my Lord Jesus Christ crucified, Son of the most blessed
Virgin Mary, open your eyes, and look upon me as you looked
from the tree of the cross upon your dear Mother sorrowing
and afflicted. *Credo.*

III

O my Lord Jesus Christ crucified, Son of the most blessed
Virgin Mary, open your blessed mouth, and speak to me as
you spoke to St John when you gave him for son to your own
most beloved Mother. *Credo.*

IV

O my Lord Jesus Christ crucified, Son of the most blessed Virgin Mary, open your arms and embrace me as you opened them upon the cross to embrace the whole human race. *Credo.*

V

O my Lord Jesus Christ crucified, Son of the most blessed Virgin Mary, open your heart and receive therein my heart, and hear me in all that I ask of you, if it be agreeable to your most holy will. *Credo.*

St Pius V

Ah, Jesus Christ our Lord God, descend among us, complete and perfect this work and bring it to the holy end that you desire.

Bd Ramón Lull

You know, Lord, that if it be pleasing to you I am ready to bear all insults and torments and even death for you. Therefore, as you know this to be the truth, have mercy on me now, for to you I commit my soul.

St Richard of Chichester

O loving Jesus, increase my patience according as my sufferings increase.

St Rita of Cascia

Lord Christ, I ask only that I might have the strength to
endure what I must.

Lord Christ, I put my trust in you that you will grant me
life beyond death.

St Saturninus

You, my creator, who for sustenance has freely given me your
flesh, who are a fire consuming the unworthy: O consume me
not! rather, enter into my body, enter into every limb, into my
very heart and veins!

Burn up, like thorns, all my transgressions! Purge my soul,
and hallow my imagination! Knit firm my bones, my joints!
Shine into all the darks of my five senses! Fasten me wholly in
the fear of you!

Guard me! shield, shelter me evermore from every word
and deed that stains the soul. Cleanse, wash, adorn me, set me
right! Give me understanding and enlighten me. Prove me the
habitation of your Spirit only, nowise the dwelling place of sin.

Forth from this house of yours, at the coming in of what I
have received, let every evil passion, every work take flight as
from a raging fire.

Praying and interceding for me are all the saints, whom
now I set before you, the princes of the bodiless orders, your
forerunner, the wise apostles, and above all your pure, your
spotless Mother: accept their prayers, my Christ, in your
compassion! Of your servant make a child of light!

For you alone, O blessed Lord, are both the enlightening
and hallowing of our souls. To you, day and day, we give
befitting glory, Master, our God. Amen.

St Symeon the New Theologian

My God, dispose of me, and of all that belongs to me,
according to your good pleasure. Amen.

St Teresa of Ávila

Make us, Lord, worthy to serve our brothers and sisters who
are scattered all over the world, who live and die alone and
poor. Give them today, using our hands, their daily bread.
And, using our love, give them peace and happiness. Amen.

Mother Teresa of Calcutta

O Jesus, who in your bitter passion became 'the reproach of
men and the man of sorrows,' I venerate your sacred
countenance in which shone the beauty and the sweetness of
the divinity, now become for my sake like the face of a 'leper'!
But in those disfigured features I recognize your infinite love,
and I long to love you and to make you loved by all men. The
tears that fall so abundantly from your eyes appear to me as
precious pearls that I love to gather, and so purchase with
their infinite value the souls of poor sinners.

O Jesus, whose face is the only beauty that ravishes my
heart, I am content not to see here below the tenderness of
your gaze, not to experience the ineffable kiss of your mouth,
but I beseech you to imprint in me your divine likeness, and
inflame me with your love so that it may consume me quickly
and I may soon behold your glorious face in heaven. Amen.

St Thérèse of Lisieux

O Jesus, I ask of you only peace!…Peace, and above all
Love—love without bound or limit. Jesus, let me for your sake
die a martyr; give me martyrdom of soul or body. Ah! rather
give me both the one and the other!

St Thérèse of Lisieux

Love!…that is what I ask.…I know but one thing now—to
love you, O Jesus!

St Thérèse of Lisieux

Souls—dear Lord, we must have souls! Above all, souls of
apostles and of martyrs, that through them we may inflame
the multitude of poor sinners with love of you.

St Thérèse of Lisieux

O my God! I offer you all my actions of this day for the
intentions and glory of the sacred heart of Jesus. I desire to
sanctify every beat of my heart, by uniting them to its infinite
merits, and I wish to make reparation for my sins by casting
them into the furnace of its merciful love. O my God! I ask
you for myself and for those whom I hold dear the grace to
fulfill perfectly your holy will, to accept for love of you the
joys and sorrows of this passing life, so that we one day may
be united in heaven for all eternity. Amen.

St Thérèse of Lisieux

O my God, most blessed Trinity, I desire to love you and to make you loved, to labour for the glory of holy Church by saving souls still on earth and by delivering those who suffer in purgatory. I desire to accomplish your will perfectly, and to attain to the degree of glory that you have prepared for me in your kingdom—in one word, I desire to be a saint, but I know that I am powerless, and I implore you, O my God, to be yourself my sanctity.

Since you have so loved me as to give me your only Son to be my saviour and my spouse, the infinite treasures of his merits are mine, to you I offer them with joy, beseeching you to see me only as in the face of Jesus and in his heart burning with love.

Again, I offer you all the merits of the saints—in heaven and on earth—their acts of love and those of the holy angels; and finally I offer you, O blessed Trinity, the love and the merits of the holy Virgin, my most dear Mother; it is to her I entrust my oblation, begging her to present it to you.

Her divine Son, my well-beloved spouse, during his life on earth, told us, 'If you ask the Father anything in my name he will give it to you.' I am then certain that you will hearken to my desires....My God, I know it, the more you will to give the more you make us desire. Immense are the desires that I feel within my heart, and it is with confidence that I call upon you to come and take possession of my soul. I cannot receive you in Holy Communion as often as I would; but, Lord, are you not Almighty?...Remain in me as in the tabernacle—never leave your little victim.

I long to console you for the ingratitude of the wicked and I pray you take from me the liberty to displease you! If through frailty I fall sometimes, may your divine glance purify my soul immediately, consuming every imperfection—like fire that transforms all things into itself....

After exile on earth I hope to enjoy the possession of you in our eternal fatherland, but I have no wish to amass merits for heaven. I will work for your love alone, my sole aim being to give you pleasure, to console your sacred heart, and to save souls who will love you forever.

At the close of life's evening I shall appear before you with empty hands, for I ask not, Lord, that you would count my works....All our justice is tarnished in your sight. It is, therefore, my desire to be clothed with your own justice and to receive from your Love the eternal possession of yourself. I crave no other throne nor other crown but you, O my beloved!...

In your sight time is nothing, one day is as a thousand years. You can in an instant prepare me to appear before you.

That I may live in one act of perfect love, I offer myself as a victim of holocaust to your merciful love, imploring you to consume me without ceasing, and to let the tide of infinite tenderness pent up in you overflow into my soul, so that I may become a very martyr of your love, O my God!

May this martyrdom, having first prepared me to appear before you, break life's thread at last, and may my soul take its flight, unretarded, into the eternal embrace of your merciful Love.

I desire, O well-beloved, at every heartbeat to renew this oblation an infinite number of times, till the shadows retire and I can tell you my love eternally face to face!

St Thérèse of Lisieux

Omnipotent Trinity,
To you be endless glory given;
Grant us eternal life with you
In our sweet fatherland of heaven. Amen.

St Thomas Aquinas

Godhead here in hiding, whom I do adore
Masked by these bare shadows, shape and nothing more,
See, Lord, at thy service low lies here a heart
Lost, all lost in wonder at the God thou art.

Seeing, touching, tasting are in thee deceived;
How says trusty hearing? that shall be believed:
What God's Son has told me, take for true I do;
Truth himself speaks truly or there's nothing true.

On the cross thy godhead made no sign to men;
Here thy very manhood steals from human ken:
Both are my confession, both are my belief,
And I pray the prayer of the dying thief.

I am not like Thomas, wounds I cannot see,
But can plainly call thee Lord and God as he:
This faith each day deeper be my holding of,
Daily make me harder hope and dearer love.

O thou our reminder of Christ crucified,
Living bread the life of us for whom he died,
Lend this life to me then: feed and feast my mind,
There be thou the sweetness man was meant to find.

Bring the tender tale true of the Pelican;
Bathe me, Jesu Lord, in what thy bosom ran—

Blood that but one drop of has the worth to win
All the world forgiveness of its world of sin.

Jesu whom I look at shrouded here below,
I beseech thee send me what I thirst for so,
Some day to gaze on thee face to face in light
And be blest for ever with thy glory's sight.

> *St Thomas Aquinas*
> *(As translated by Gerard Manley Hopkins)*

Grant me, O merciful God, that what is pleasing to you I may
ardently examine, truthfully acknowledge, and perfectly
accomplish for the praise and glory of your name. Regulate my
whole life, O God, and let me know your will that I may fulfil
it; give me the grace to do that which is necessary and
profitable for my soul. Grant, O Lord my God, that I may not
fail in prosperity or in adversity, avoiding pride in the former
and discouragement in the latter. May I rejoice in nothing but
what leads to you, grieve for nothing but what turns away
from you. May I wish to please no one but you, and fear to
displease no one but you.

May I despise, O Lord, all transitory things, and prize only
that which is eternal. May I shun any joy that is not you; may I
wish for nothing outside of you. May I delight in any work
undertaken for you, and tire of any repose that is without you.
Grant me, O my God, to direct my heart toward you,
constantly to grieve for my sins, and to amend my life.

Make me, O Lord, my God, obedient without
contradiction, poor without depression, chaste without
corruption, patient without murmuring, humble without
pretence, cheerful without dissipation, sorrowful without

despair, serious without constraint, prompt without levity, God-fearing without presumption, correcting my neighbour without haughtiness, and edifying him by word and example without hypocrisy.

Give me, O Lord God, a watchful heart, which no curious thought will turn away from you; a noble heart, which no unworthy affection will drag down; a righteous heart, which no irregular intention will turn aside; a firm heart, which no tribulation will crush; a free heart, which no violent affection will claim for its own.

Grant me, finally, O Lord my God, intelligence in knowing you, diligence in seeking you, wisdom in finding you, perseverance in trusting you, and the confidence of finally embracing you. Let me accept your punishments as a penance for my sins, and enjoy your benefits by grace in this world, and your blessedness by glory in the next. Who lives and reigns true God, for ever and ever. Amen.

St Thomas Aquinas

O ineffable Creator, who out of the depths of your wisdom appointed three hierarchies of angels, and placed them in wonderful harmony above your empyrean heaven, and orders most perfectly your whole creation; you, who are the true fountain and highest source of light and wisdom, shed a ray of your brightness upon the darkness of my intellect, taking from me that twofold darkness of sin and ignorance in which I was born.

O you, who makes the tongues of little ones eloquent, instruct my tongue, and pour upon my lips the grace of your blessing. Give me keenness of comprehension, ability to retain, method and ease in acquiring, precision in interpreting, plenteous grace in speaking. Inspire my going in; guide my steps when I walk; and my going out make perfect. You who are at once God and man, and who reign forever and ever. Amen.

St Thomas Aquinas

O God, all powerful, who knows all things, who had neither beginning nor end, who gives, preserves, and rewards all virtues; deign to make me steadfast on the solid foundation of *faith,* to protect me with the impregnable shield of *hope,* and to adorn me with the wedding garment of *charity.*

St Thomas Aquinas

Give me *justice,* to submit to you; *prudence,* to avoid the snares of the enemy; *temperance,* to keep the just medium; *fortitude,* to bear adversities with patience.

St Thomas Aquinas

Grant me to impart willingly to others whatever I possess that is good, and to ask humbly of others that I may partake of the good of which I am destitute; to confess truly my faults; to bear with equanimity the pains and evils that I suffer. Grant that I may never envy the good of my neighbour, and that I may always return thanks for your graces.

Let me always observe discipline in my clothing, movements, and gestures. Let my tongue be restrained from vain words, my feet from going astray, my eyes from seeking after vain objects, my ears from listening to much news; may I humbly incline my countenance, and raise my spirit to heaven.

Grant me to despise all transitory things, and to desire you alone; to subdue my flesh and purify my conscience; to honour your saints, and to praise you worthily; to advance in virtue, and to end good actions by a happy death.

Plant in me, O Lord, all virtues: that I may be devoted to divine things, provident in human affairs, and troublesome to no one in bodily cares.

Grant me, O Lord, fervour in contrition, sincerity in confession, and completeness in satisfaction.

Deign to direct my soul to a good life: that what I do may be pleasing to you, meritorious for myself, and edifying to my neighbour.

Grant that I may never desire to do what is foolish, and that I may never be discouraged by what is distasteful; that I may never begin my works before the proper time, nor abandon them before they are completed. Amen.

St Thomas Aquinas

Dearest Jesus! I know well that every perfect gift, and above all others that of chastity, depends upon the most powerful assistance of your providence, and that without you a creature can do nothing. Therefore, I pray you to defend with your grace, chastity and purity in my soul as well as in my body. And if I have ever received the impression of anything sensible that can stain my chastity and purity, take it from me, supreme Lord of all my powers, that I may with a pure heart advance in your love and service, offering myself chaste all the days of my life on the most pure altar of your divinity. Amen.

St Thomas Aquinas

O almighty and eternal God, behold I draw near to the Sacrament of your only begotten Son, our Lord Jesus Christ. I come as one sick to the physician of life, as one unclean to the source of all mercy, as one blind to the light of the eternal sun; as one poor and needy to the Lord of heaven and earth.

I beseech you, therefore, out of the abundance of your unspeakable goodness, to heal my infirmity, cleanse me from the dross of sin, illumine my blindness, enrich my poverty, clothe my nakedness, that I may receive the bread of angels, the King of kings, the Lord of lords, with such reverence and humility, such contrition and devotion, such purity and faith, such uprightness of purpose and intention as may be profitable to the salvation of my soul.

Grant me, I beseech you, O Lord, to receive not only your body and blood, but also the grace and virtue of this Sacrament.

O most merciful God, grant me so to receive the body of your only Son, our Lord Jesus Christ, which he took of Mary ever Virgin, that I may merit to be incorporated with his mystical body and numbered among his members. O most loving Father, as yet a wayfarer upon earth, I am about to welcome into my heart your own beloved Son now hidden beneath the sacramental veil; may I at length contemplate him face-to-face forever; who with you lives and reigns in the unity of the Holy Spirit, God, world without end. Amen.

St Thomas Aquinas

I render thanks to you, O Lord, Holy Father, everlasting God,
who have vouchsafed, not for any merits of mine, but of your
great mercy only, to feed me a sinner, your unworthy servant,
with the precious body and blood of your Son, our Lord Jesus
Christ; and I pray that this Holy Communion may not be for
my judgment and condemnation, but for my pardon and
salvation. Let it be unto me an armour of faith and a shield of
good purpose, a riddance of all vices, and a rooting out of all
evil desires; an increase of love and patience, of humility and
obedience, and of all virtues; a firm defence against the wiles
of all my enemies, visible and invisible; a perfect quieting of all
my impulses, fleshly and spiritual; a cleaving unto you, the
one true God; and a blessed consummation of my end when
you call. And I pray that you would vouchsafe to bring me a
sinner to that unspeakable feast where you, with your Son and
your Holy Spirit, are to your holy ones true light, full
blessedness, everlasting joy, and perfect happiness. Through
the same Christ our Lord. Amen.

St Thomas Aquinas

O triune Deity, to you we pray,
Honoured upon the altar day by day,
Visit our souls, and by your holy light
Lead us to heaven, and be your paths our way. Amen.

St Thomas Aquinas

Let my prayer be directed, O Lord, as incense in your sight;
the lifting up of my hands as an evening sacrifice. Set a watch,
O Lord, before my mouth: and a door round about my lips;
that my heart may not incline to evil words: to make excuses
in sins.

Psalm 140(141):2-4

May the Lord enkindle in us the fire of his love and the flame
of everlasting charity. Amen.

Incensation prayer from the Old Mass

Good Lord, give me the grace, in all my fear and agony, to
have recourse to that great fear and wonderful agony that
thou, my sweet Saviour, hadst at the Mount of Olivet before
thy most bitter passion, and in the meditation thereof to
conceive ghostly comfort and consolation profitable for my
soul.

Almighty God, take from me all vain glorious minds, all
appetites of mine own praise, all envy, covetise, gluttony,
sloth, and lechery, all wrathful affections, all appetite of
revenging, all desire or delight of other folk's harm, all
pleasure in provoking any person to wrath and anger, all
delight of exprobation or insultation against any person in
their affliction and calamity.

And give me, good Lord, an humble, lowly, quiet,
peaceable, patient, charitable, kind, tender, and pitiful mind
with all my works, and all my words, and all my thoughts, to
have a taste of thy holy, blessed Spirit.

Give me, good Lord, a full faith, a firm hope, and a fervent charity, a love to the good Lord incomparable above the love to myself; and that I love nothing to thy displeasure, but everything in an order to thee.

Give me, good Lord, a longing to be with thee, not for the avoiding of the calamities of this wretched world, nor so much for the avoiding of the pains of purgatory, nor of the pains of hell neither, nor so much for the attaining of the joys of heaven in respect of mine own commodity, as even for a very love to thee.

And bear me, good Lord, thy love and favour, which thing my love to thee-ward, were it never so great, could not, but of thy great goodness deserve.

And pardon me, good Lord, that I am so bold to ask so high petitions, being so vile a sinful wretch, and so unworthy to attain the lowest. Put yet, good Lord, such they be as I am bounden to wish, and should be nearer the effectual desire of them if my manifold sins were not the let. From which, O glorious Trinity, vouchsafe, of thy goodness to wash me with that blessed blood that issued out of thy tender body, O sweet saviour Christ, in the divers torment of thy most bitter passion.

Take from me, good Lord, this lukewarm fashion, or rather key-cold manner of meditation, and this dullness in praying unto thee. And give me warmth, delight, and quickness in thinking upon thee. And give me thy grace to long for thine holy sacraments, and specially to rejoice in the presence of thy very blessed body, sweet saviour Christ, in the holy sacrament of the altar, and duly to thank thee for thy gracious visitation therewith, and at that high memorial with tender compassion to remember and consider thy most bitter passion.

Make us all, good Lord, virtually participant of that holy sacrament this day, and every day. Make us all lively members, sweet saviour Christ, of thine holy mystical body, thy Catholic Church.

Vouchsafe, O Lord, this day, to keep us from sin. Have mercy on us, O Lord, have mercy on us.

Let thy mercy, O Lord, be upon us, as we have trusted in thee.

In thee, O Lord, have I hoped, let me not be confounded forever.

St Thomas More

Give me thy grace to amend my life and to have an eye to mine end without grudge of death, which to them that die in thee, good Lord, is the gate of a wealthy life.

St Thomas More

Almighty God, have mercy on N. and N., and on all that bear me evil will, and would me harm, and their faults and mine together by such easy, tender, merciful means as thine infinite wisdom best can devise, vouchsafe to amend and redress and make us saved souls in heaven together, where we may ever live and love together with thee and thy blessed saints, O glorious Trinity, for the bitter passion of our sweet saviour Christ. Amen.

St Thomas More

For joys of service, you we praise,
whose favour crowneth all our days;
For humble tasks that bring delight,
when done, O Lord, as in your sight.
Accept our offerings, Lord most high,
our work, our purpose sanctify,
and with our gifts may we have place,
now in the Kingdom of your grace.

St Venantius

Lord Jesus Christ, who want none to perish, to whom all
appeal with hope of mercy—for you said yourself, 'Whatever
you ask the Father in my name, that I will do'—I beg of you in
your name that in my dying moments you give me full use of
my senses and speech; profound, heartfelt contrition for my
sins; firm faith; hope in good measure; and perfect love, that I
may be able to say to you with a pure heart, 'Into your hands,
O Lord, I commend my spirit. You have redeemed me, Lord
God of truth, who are blessed and full of glory for ever and
ever. Amen.'

St Vincent Ferrer

Truly, O Lord, you have become our refuge: to you have I fled;
teach me your will and make me do it…I am yours: O save
me. Into your hands I commend my spirit. By your grace I will
not forsake you.

Bd William of Saint Thierry

Prayers
of
Thanksgiving

O tender Father, you gave me more, much more than I ever thought to ask for. I realize that our human desires can never really match what you long to give us.

Thanks, and again thanks, O Father, for having granted my petitions, and that which I never realized I needed or petitioned. Amen.

St Catherine of Siena

Thank you, good Jesus, your mercies are above all your works.

St Aelred of Rievaulx

I thank you, Lord Jesus Christ, for your goodness in accepting me, an offering by fire for your name's sake: for you offered yourself upon the cross as a sacrifice for the sins of all the world.

I offer myself in death to you, who live and reign with the Father and the Holy Spirit, ages without end. Amen.

St Afra

O my God! I give you thanks for allowing me time to amend, now that it is the time of mercy and not of punishment. I would rather lose all things than forfeit your grace.

St Alphonsus de' Liguori

Thanks be to you, my joy and my glory and my confidence, my God, thanks be to you for your gifts; but do preserve them for me. For so will you preserve me, and those things shall be enlarged and perfected that you have given me, and I myself shall be with you, since even to be you have given me.

St Augustine

Late have I loved you, O eternal truth and goodness: late have I sought you, my Father!

But you sought me, and when you shone forth upon me, then I knew you, then I learned, so late, to love you.

I thank you, O my light, that you taught my soul what you

would be to me, and inclined your face to me in pity. You, O Lord, have become my hope, my comfort, my strength, my all: my soul rejoices in you. The darkness vanished from before my eyes, and I beheld you, the sun of righteousness!

When I loved darkness, then I knew you not, but wandered on from night to night. But you led me out at last from that blindness. You took me by my hand, and you called me, then, to you.

And now I can thank you, and your mighty voice, which has penetrated to my inmost heart. Amen.

St Augustine

And since it is not profitable for us
To be silent and restrained,
Let our infirmity render to you
The song of our thanksgiving.
You good! who does not exact
More than our ability,
How will your servant be condemned
Both in principal and interest,
Should he not give what he is able,
But hold back what he owes!
O you sea of glory,
Who needs not to be glorified!
Receive in your goodness
The drop of thanksgiving:—
You, who has by your gift
Harmonized my tongue for your praise!

St Ephrem the Syrian

For this, O Christ, I thank you. Keep me in your care, for I am suffering, owing to my faith in you. I worship the Father, the Son, and the Holy Spirit. I worship the Holy Trinity, apart from you there is no other God. For this, O Christ, I thank you.

Lord, the glory you receive from those whom you in your mercy have summoned is great. Lord, protect all of your servants: remain with them until the end, for then they will glorify your name for all eternity.

For this, Lord Jesus Christ, I give you thanks: your strength has sustained me; you have kept my soul from perishing; you have granted to me grace, the grace of your name. Now complete that which has been begun in me and by this put the Adversary to shame.

St Euplus

Almighty, most holy, most high and supreme God, holy and just Father, Lord King of heaven and earth, for yourself we give thanks to you because by your holy will, and by your only Son, you have created all things spiritual and corporal in the Holy Spirit and placed us made to your image and likeness in paradise, whence we fell by our own fault. And we give you thanks because, as by your Son you created us, so by the true and holy love with which you have loved us, you caused him, true God and true man, to be born of the glorious and ever-Virgin, most blessed Holy Mary, and willed that he should redeem us captives by his cross and blood and death. And we give thanks to you because your Son himself is to come again in the glory of his majesty to put the wicked who have not done penance for their sins, and have not known you, in eternal fire, and to say to all who have known you and adored you, and served you in penance: 'Come, you blessed of my Father, possess the kingdom prepared for you from the beginning of the world.'

And since all we wretches and sinners are not worthy to name you, we humbly beseech you, that our Lord Jesus Christ, your beloved Son, in whom you are well pleased, together with the Holy Spirit, the Paraclete, may give thanks to you as it is pleasing to you and them, for all; he suffices you always for all through whom you have done so much for us. Alleluia. And we earnestly beg the glorious Mother, the most Blessed Mary ever-Virgin, Blessed Michael, Gabriel, Raphael, and all the choirs of the blessed spirits, seraphim, cherubim, and thrones, dominations, principalities and powers, virtues, angels and archangels, blessed John the Baptist, John the Evangelist, Peter, Paul, the blessed patriarchs and prophets, innocents, apostles, evangelists, disciples, martyrs, confessors, virgins, blessed Elias and Enoch, and all the saints who have been and are, and shall be, for your love, that they may, as it is pleasing to you, give thanks for these things to the most high, true God, eternal and living, with your most dear Son, our Lord Jesus Christ, and the Holy Spirit, the Paraclete, for ever and ever. Amen. Alleluia.

St Francis of Assisi

I kiss the hand of your providence; I entrust myself fully and completely to your guidance. Heavenly Father, do with me as you will. It pleases you, O Lord, to lead me along wondrous ways. But who can know your paths and plans? Behold your servant! send me where you will! Like a child I fly to your embrace: carry me. It pleases you to lead me along a road beset by adversities, obstacles, and difficulties; for this I thank you, I thank you very much. I believe that as I travel this road I will not easily lose my way because it is the road taken by my beloved redeemer, Jesus Christ.

Bd George Matulaitis

May my heart and my soul, with all the substance of my flesh, all my senses, and all the powers of my body and my mind, with all creatures, praise you and give you thanks, O sweetest Lord, faithful lover of humanity, for your signal mercy.

St Gertrude of Helfta

I adore and bless with thanksgiving, and with all humility, your ineffable charity, O Father of mercies, by which, notwithstanding the disorders of my life, you have had thoughts of peace toward me, and not of severity, overwhelming me with the greatness and multitude of your benefits, even as if I had led the life of an angel among men.

St Gertrude of Helfta

We praise and thank you, O God, through your Son, Jesus Christ, our Lord, through whom you have enlightened us, by revealing the light that never fades.

Night is falling and day's allotted span draws to a close. The daylight that you created for your pleasure has fully satisfied us; and yet, of your own free gift, now the evening lights do not fail us.

We praise you and glorify you through your Son, Jesus Christ, our Lord. Amen.

St Hippolytus

I thank you, Lord and Master, that you have deemed to
honour me by making complete my love for you in that you
have bound me with chains of iron to your apostle Paul.

St Ignatius of Antioch

I give you thanks, Lord Jesus Christ: In the midst of my trials
and suffering you have granted me the strength not to waver;
by your mercy, you have given me a share of glory eternal.

St Irenaeus of Sirmium

May you be praised, Lord God, for the printed word, bread for
our minds, light for our lives.

We give thanks for the talents and dedication of all who
serve the truth in love and for all whose administration and
technical skills make possible the production of books,
newspapers, magazines, and reviews.

We celebrate, Lord, the modern marvel of television, which
brings into the hearts of our homes the joys and pain of all
human living. Music, drama, and laughter are shared in ways
undreamed of in the past.

May you be praised, Lord God, for the radio, which soars
on the wings of the wind and provides for each nation an
immediate channel for news, views, and entertainment and a
means of offering to the listening world its own distinctive
voice.

We celebrate, Lord, the writers, artists, directors, and all
those whose gifts light up both theatre and cinema and
provide audiences with heightened awareness of their human
condition.

We thank you, Lord God, for the unending Pentecost of your creative Holy Spirit, which enables your sons and daughters to catch fire from your truth, beauty, and goodness.

We celebrate the wonder of digital communications manifesting a new iconography that can link people around the globe in solidarity of faith, hope, and love.

May the blind see, the deaf hear, the poor have the Good News proclaimed to them by all who rejoice in their God-given talents and their gift of creativity. Amen.

Ven. James Alberione

It is suitable and right to hymn you, to bless you, to praise you, to give thanks to you, to worship you, in every part of your dominion. For you are God, ineffable, inconceivable, invisible, incomprehensible, the same from everlasting to everlasting; you and your only-begotten Son, and the Holy Spirit. For you brought us forth to being from nothing, and when we had fallen raised us up again, and gave not over until you had done every thing that you might bring us to heaven, and bestow on us your kingdom to come. For all these things we give thanks to you, and to your only-begotten Son, and your Holy Spirit, for your benefits that we know, and that we know not, manifest and concealed, which you have bestowed upon us.

St John Chrysostom

We render thanks unto you, O King invisible, who framed all things by your measureless power, and in the multitude of your mercy have brought all things into being from nonexistence.

St John Chrysostom

My God, I thank you with all my heart for all the graces you have bestowed on me during my whole life, and especially for those of this day. Amen.

St Louis Marie Grignion de Montfort

My God, I offer you the heart of your beloved Son to serve as an act of thanksgiving for the blessings that I have received from you, for my prayer, for my offering, for my adoration, and for all my resolutions. Receive them, eternal Father, to supply whatever is wanting in me since I have nothing to offer that is worthy of you, except Jesus, my saviour, whom you have given me to possess and to enjoy. Amen.

St Margaret Mary Alacoque

I have received of you a joy unmixed with pain. O Lord, receive my rejoicing and singing of your mercy and compassion. You have given me this joy of heart. I render to you with gladness my tribute of thanksgiving.

St Methodius

Lord, I give thanks to you for your dying on the cross for my sins.

St Paul of the Cross

O Lord, I rejoice in my total dependence on you. Command what you will and help me ever to praise you by saying, 'Thanks be to God!'

Bd Pauline von Mallinckrodt

I thank you, O Lord Jesus, for all the benefits you have bestowed on me, and for the pains and ignominy you suffered for my sake, on account of which that sad complaint of the prophet, 'There is no sorrow like my sorrow,' truly applied to you.

St Richard of Chichester

It has pleased you, Lord, to keep me until this time. I thought, for a while, that you had rejected me as being a stone not fit for your building; but now that you call me to take my place in it, I am ready to suffer that I may have a part in your kingdom with all your saints.

St Serenus

I worship you, O Christ, and I thank you that I have been counted worthy to suffer for your name.

St Theodota of Philippopolis

Lord Jesus Christ, creator of heaven and earth; you will never abandon those who put their trust in you.

We give you thanks: you have prepared us to live in your heavenly city and share in your kingdom.

We give you thanks: you have strengthened us to overcome the serpent and crush its head.

Grant rest to your servants, let the violence of their enemies be placed upon me.

Grant peace to your Church; may it be delivered from the oppression of the Wicked One.

St Theodotus of Ancyra

I thank you, O my God, for all the graces you have bestowed
on me, and particularly for making me pass through the
crucible of suffering. It is with joy I shall behold you on the
last day bearing your sceptre—the cross. Since you have
deigned to give me for my portion this most precious cross, I
have hope of resembling you in heaven and seeing the sacred
stigmata of your passion shine in my glorified body.

St Thérèse of Lisieux

I praise you, I glorify you, I bless you, O God, for the immense
blessings you have given me, notwithstanding my
unworthiness.

I bless your clemency in waiting for me, your sweetness in
correcting instead of destroying me, your tenderness in calling
me, your benignity in receiving me, your mercy in pardoning
me, your goodness in filling me with favours, your patience in
forgetting my injuries, your humility in consoling me, your
compassion in protecting me, your eternity in preserving me,
and your truth in rewarding me.

How shall I speak, my God, of your ineffable goodness? For
when a fugitive, you call me back; returning, you receive me;
stumbling, you bear me up; despairing, you fill me with joy;
negligent, you spur me on; fighting, you arm me; conquering,
you crown me, a sinner. You do not spurn me after
repentance, and you remember not my offences. You deliver
me from many dangers, soften my heart to penance, make me
fearful by punishments, allure me by rewards, chastise me by
scourges, and guard me by the ministry of angels. You give me
earthly goods, while you reserve for me those that are eternal.
You encourage me by your dignity of creation, you draw me to

yourself by the clemency of redemption, and you promise me the rewards of sanctification.

I am unable to offer you fitting praises for all these benefits. But I return thanks to your Majesty for the abundance of your infinite goodness, and I beseech you that you will ever increase grace in me, that after increasing it, you will preserve it, and after preserving it, you will reward it. Amen.

St Thomas Aquinas

We hold as a gift more precious than gold, your love. From the beginning of creation your Son, the eternal Word, has been tossing about on the stormy waters of human souls, striving to bring peace through the gift of love. Now he has breathed over the waters of our souls, and the waves are calm. Merciful Father, we thank you.

Bd William of Saint Thierry

BIOGRAPHICAL NOTES AND INDEX

St Aelred of Rievaulx, 1110–1167: A Cistercian monk, he was abbot of Revesby in Lincolnshire and then of Rievaulx. The author of 'On Spiritual Friendship' and 'The Mirror of Charity,' he was known for his gentleness with his monks. See pages 2, 42–43, 88, 182.

St Afra, ?–304: From Augsburg, she was probably a victim of Diocletian's persecutions. See page 182.

St Agatha, ?: Little is known about her except that she was martyred in Sicily. See page 2.

Bd Aloysius Guanella, 1842–1915: Born in Fraciscio, Italy, a zealous apostle of charity, he founded the Congregations of the Daughters of St Mary of Providence and the Servants of Charity to aid the most abandoned and needy. He also established the Pious Union of the Death of St Joseph for the dying. See pages 2, 43.

St Alphonsus de' Liguori, 1696–1787: Born in Naples, he gave up a successful career as a lawyer to become a priest. He founded the Congregation of the Most Holy Redeemer, known as the Redemptorists. He is a Doctor of the Church. See pages 2–3, 43–46, 89–92, 182.

St Ambrose, c. 340–397: Born in Gaul, he became a barrister in Rome and was appointed governor of Liguria and Aemilia, with headquarters at Milan. Called to be bishop by popular acclamation, although only a catechumen, he was one of the greatest and most beloved bishops of all time. He is a Doctor of the Church. See page 46.

St Anselm of Canterbury, c. 1033–1109: From Aosta, in Italy, he became abbot of Bec in France and later archbishop of Canterbury in England. Because of conflicts with the English kings, Anselm went twice into exile. He is known as the Father of Scholastic Theology and is a Doctor of the Church. See pages 47–48, 93–95.

St Anthony Mary Claret, 1807–1870: Appointed archbishop of Santiago de Cuba, he was also confessor to Queen Isabella II and was exiled with her during the revolution of 1868. He is the founder of the Missionary Sons of the Immaculate Heart of Mary ('Claretians'). See pages 48, 95.

St Anthony of Padua, 1195–1231: Born in Lisbon, he left the Augustinians to become a Franciscan. Ill health forced him to abandon his missionary activities among the Moors, and during his return voyage from Morocco a storm brought him to Italy, where he remained. He was a famous preacher—undoubtedly one of the greatest of all times—and was reputedly visited by the child Jesus. He is a Doctor of the Church. See pages 95–96.

Bd Arnold Janssen, 1837–1909: This German priest founded the Society of the Divine Word, the Holy Spirit Missionary Sisters, and the cloistered branch of Perpetual Adoration. He opened the first house for training missionaries in the United States in 1908. See pages 3–4, 96.

St Augustine, 354–430: Born in Thagaste, in North Africa, he experienced a singular conversion in Milan, famously recounted in his autobiography *Confessions*. As bishop of Hippo, he found himself constantly opposing one heresy or another. This Doctor of the Church and greatest of the Latin Fathers is also known for his *City of God*. See pages 4–5, 49, 96–99, 182–83.

St Basil the Great, 329–379: Born at Caesarea in Cappadocia, he is one of the greatest of all bishops, having defended his huge see of Caesarea against the Arian heresy. Because he established the first monastery in Asia Minor, he is regarded as the father of all Eastern monks. See pages 49, 99–100.

St Benedict, c. 480–c. 547: Born in Umbria, Italy, he fled from the licence of Rome and lived as a hermit at Subiaco, where he attracted a number of disciples. He founded the monastery of Monte Cassino, for whose monks he wrote the rule that bears his name. That rule spread throughout Europe and became the norm for all Western monks. See pages 49–50, 101.

St Benedict Joseph Labre, 1748–1783: Born in France, he embarked on foot upon a series of pilgrimages to the chief shrines of Western Europe, depending upon divine providence for his needs. From 1774 until his death he lived in Rome, spending his days in the churches and his nights in the ruins of the Colosseum. See page 51.

St Bernadette Soubirous of Lourdes, 1854–1879: God chose this child to reveal to the world the healing shrine of Our Lady of Lourdes in France. She suffered much on account of her visions of the Blessed Virgin Mary and joined the Sisters of Notre Dame at Nevers to keep out of the public eye. See pages 5, 52, 101–2.

St Bernard of Clairvaux, 1090–1153: Born in Dijon, France, he formed and became abbot of Clairvaux, the fourth house of the order of Cîteaux. During his lifetime he established sixty-eight Cistercian monasteries, advised popes, and preached against heresy. He is a Doctor of the Church. See pages 5–7, 52.

St Bernardine of Siena, 1380–1444: A great preacher, he restored strict observance in the Franciscan order, especially in the matter of poverty. Called 'the people's preacher,' he spread devotion to the Holy Name of Jesus. See pages 7, 102–3.

St Birgitta, 1303–1373: Married, she had eight children, of whom one, Catherine, is also a saint. Birgitta became chief lady-in-waiting to the queen of Magnus II, king of Sweden, and received remarkable visions and revelations. She died in Rome, the adviser of popes and kings. See pages 7–8, 104.

St Bonaventure, 1221–1274: Born near Viterbo, he was elected minister general of the Franciscans and was made cardinal-bishop of Albano. Among the greatest scholastics of the Middle Ages, he laboured for unity among the friars of his order. He is a Doctor of the Church. See pages 52–54, 104–5.

St Boris of Kiev, ?–1015: He and his brother Gleb were murdered by their brother Svyatopolk. Because they accepted an unjust death without resistance, they are revered as martyrs. See page 105.

St Brigid, c. 450–c. 525: Among the most venerated of Irish saints, she was born in Faughart, became a nun at an early age, and founded the monastery of Kildare, becoming the spiritual mother of Irish nuns for many centuries. See page 105.

St Catherine dei Ricci, 1522–1590: Born in Florence, she became a regular tertiary of St Dominic. She had an extraordinary series of ecstasies in which she beheld and enacted the scenes of our Lord's passion. She is said to have had the stigmata and to have received the spiritual espousals. See pages 105–6.

St Catherine of Genoa, 1447–1510: Married at the age of sixteen, she underwent a sudden conversion at the age of twenty-six and gave herself to the care of the sick in hospital. She is a remarkable example of complete otherworldliness united with capable practicality. She wrote *Dialogue between the Soul and the Body* and *Treatise on Purgatory*. See pages 9, 54.

St Catherine of Siena, 1347–1380: One of the greatest women of Christendom, she persuaded Pope Gregory XI to abandon Avignon for Rome. She also wrote a great mystical work, her *Dialogue*. She is a Doctor of the Church. See pages 9, 54, 106–8, 181.

St Clare of Assisi, c. 1193–1253: Having run away from home to join St Francis, she helped establish the first convent of Franciscan nuns, now called after her Poor Clares. She was successful in restoring communal poverty for her community. See pages 55–56.

St Claude de la Colombière, 1641–1682: A Jesuit, he was St Margaret Mary's coadjutor in propagating devotion to the Sacred Heart of Jesus. See pages 9–10.

St Clement Maria Hofbauer, 1751–1820: From Tasswitz, Moravia, he worked as a baker, became a hermit, and joined the Redemptorists. He went as a missionary to Warsaw, working among the poor and building orphanages and schools. Expelled by Napoleon, he returned to Vienna, eventually establishing a Catholic college and revitalizing the religious life of the German nations. He is patron of Vienna. See pages 10, 108–9.

St Clement of Alexandria, second century: Born in Athens, he became master of the Christian school of doctrine in Alexandria, where he taught St Alexander and Origen. He is a Doctor in the Roman Liturgy. See page 109.

St Clement of Rome, ?–c. 99: According to tradition, he succeeded Cletus as pope in 91, was exiled to the Crimea by Emperor Trajan, and preached the faith so zealously among the prisoners that he was condemned to death and thrown into the sea with an anchor tied to his neck. See pages 87, 109–10.

St Columba, c. 521–597: Probably born in County Donegal, Ireland, he built on the island of Iona, off the coast of Scotland, a monastery that grew into the greatest in Christendom. The monastic rule he developed was practiced widely all over Europe. See page 110.

St Columbanus, c. 540–615: Born in West Leinster, Ireland, he was sent as a missionary to Gaul and built the famous monastery of Luxeuil. He also established the famous abbey of Bobbio. See pages 111–12.

Bd Crescentia Höss, ?–1744: Initially neglected because she did not bring a dowry, she was eventually made novice mistress and then superior of the house of Franciscan regular tertiaries at Kaufbeuren. See page 112.

St Crispina, ?–304: An African woman of rank, she was married, with several children. When she refused to sacrifice to the Roman gods she was beheaded. See page 112.

St Cyprian of Carthage, c. 200–258: Bishop of Carthage, he was arrested under Valerian and beheaded for the faith. See page 113.

St Cyril, ?–869: A priest in Greece, he was sent with his brother, Methodius, into Moravia as a missionary. He died in Rome. See page 113.

St Cyril of Alexandria, c. 376– 444: Born in Alexandria, he became archbishop of that city. For defending the faith against the Nestorian heresy, he is a Doctor of the Church. See page 113.

St Dativus, ?–304: A senator, he was arrested with St Saturninus and died with him in prison. See page 114.

St Dimitrii of Rostov, 1651–1709: A great hierarch, preacher, writer, ascetic, and light of the Russian Church, he was born near Kiev, became bishop (metropolitan) of Rostov, and was renowned for his translation of the Lives of the Saints. See page 114.

St Dionysius of Alexandria, died 265: Born in Arabia Felix, he was head of the catechetical school in Alexandria and became bishop. During the persecution of Decius, he governed his diocese from Libya. He was very active against the Novatian controversy. See page 114.

Bd Edith Stein, 1891–1942: A brilliant scholar, she converted from Judaism to Catholicism and later became a Carmelite nun in Cologne. She escaped to Holland when German persecution of the Jews began in 1938, but in 1942 she was deported to Auschwitz, where she died in the gas chambers. See pages 10–13, 115.

St Edmund Rich of Abingdon, 1180–1240: Having taught theology at Oxford and preached the Crusade in England, he was elected archbishop of Canterbury. His resistance to the encroachments of royal powers involved him in trouble with King Henry III. See page 116.

St Elizabeth Ann Bayley Seton, 1774–1821: Born in New York, she married and became involved in social work, helping to found the Society for the Relief of Poor Widows with Small Children. Widowed, with five children to raise, she became Catholic, was ostracized by her family, and moved to Baltimore. The school she founded was the beginning of the far-reaching Catholic school system in the United States. She was also the first superior of her order, the Sisters of Charity, the first American religious society. She is the first American-born saint. See pages 13, 57, 116–17.

Bd Elizabeth of the Trinity, 1880–1906: She entered the Carmel at Dijon, France, at the age of twenty and spent most of her short time there moving toward the fulfilment of her special calling, to become an indwelling of the Divine. See pages 14, 117–19.

St Ephrem the Syrian, c. 306–c. 379: Born in Nisibis, in Mesopotamia, he became the greatest theologian, preacher, and poet of the Syrian Church. One of the first writers of hymns, he also wrote commentaries on the Scriptures. He is a Doctor of the Church. See pages 14, 57–60, 119–21, 183.

St Euplus, ?–304: A deacon in Catania, Sicily, he was seized with a copy of the gospels on him. Refusing under torture to sacrifice to the Roman gods, he was beheaded. See page 184.

St Ferreolus of Vienne, ?: Little is known of him except that he was put to death for the faith near Vienne on the Rhône. See page 14.

St Frances Cabrini, 1850–1917: Born in Italy, she is the first U.S. citizen to be canonized. She founded the Missionary Sisters of the Sacred Heart at Codogno, Italy, then came to the United States to work with Italian immigrants, in New York and Chicago. She extended her work to Nicaragua, Costa Rica, Chile, Brazil, and Argentina. See pages 15, 121–24.

St Francis de Sales, 1567–1622: From his native Savoy he was sent as a missionary to the Protestants in the Chablais. On the basis of his success, he was eventually made bishop of Geneva. With St Jane Frances de Chantal he founded the order of Visitation Nuns. He is a Doctor of the Church, and his works include *Treatise on the Love of God* and *Introduction to the Devout Life*. See pages 15, 60–61, 125–26.

Ven. Francis Libermann, 1802–1852: The son of a rabbi, he converted but was barred from the priesthood by his epilepsy. Nevertheless, he was retained as a spiritual adviser and novice master of the Eudists. Ordained at the age of thirty-nine, he took control over the missions in West Africa. He was elected superior general of the Congregation of the Holy Spirit, and his commentary on the Gospel of St John is considered on a par with the writings of St John of the Cross and St Teresa of Ávila. See pages 61–62, 124.

St Francis Xavier, 1506–1552: Born a nobleman in Navarre, he became the second of St Ignatius Loyola's original seven followers. He was a successful missionary in India, Ceylon, Malaya, and Japan. He is the patron of foreign missions. See pages 15, 125.

St Francis of Assisi, c. 1181–1226: The son of a wealthy merchant, he spent his youth in seeking pleasure but renounced all worldly goods and founded the order of Friars Minor. He was the first to bear the stigmata, the wounds of Christ's Passion. See pages 16–18, 126, 184–85.

St Fulgentius, 468–533: From Africa, he became bishop of Ruspe but was banished by the Vandals to Sardinia. He wrote a number of treatises, especially against Arianism. See pages 126–27.

St Gabriel Possenti, 1838–1862: Born in Spoleto, Italy, he took the name Gabriel-of-Our-Lady-of-Sorrows upon entering the Passionists. His short life was marked by extraordinary effort to attain perfection in and by small things and continual cheerfulness. See pages 62–63, 127.

St Gemma Galgani, 1878–1903: Born in Tuscany, she suffered both physically and spiritually. She often experienced ecstasies and bore periodically recurring stigmata. See pages 18, 63, 127–28.

Bd George Matulaitis, 1871–1927: Born in Lithuania, he secretly restored the Marians of the Immaculate Conception in 1909 after the czar banned all religious orders in the Russian Empire. Later consecrated bishop of Vilnius, he resigned to serve as apostolic visitator for Lithuania under Pope Pius XI, and he prepared the concordat with Lithuania and the Holy See. See pages 63, 128, 185–86.

St Gertrude of Helfta, ?–1302: Gifted with supernatural revelations, she was a woman of great intellectual ability. She is the author of the work commonly called *The Revelations of St Gertrude*. See pages 19, 64–66, 128–29, 186.

St Gregory the Great, c. sixth century–604: The first monk to become pope, he sent St Augustine to convert the English, encouraged monasticism, maintained the primacy of the Roman see in East and West, enforced the discipline of the clergy, and wrote many works, including the famous *Dialogues* and a book of homilies on the gospels. He is a Doctor of the Church. See pages 66, 130.

St Gregory Nazianzen, c. 329–390: Born in Cappadocia, he read law for ten years in Athens but joined St Basil and was later ordained. Consecrated bishop, he refused a diocese, but then reluctantly accepted the see of Constantinople. After a few months he resigned and retired. For his writings, particularly directed against Arianism, he is a Doctor of the Church. See pages 67, 129.

St Henry de Osso, 1840–1896: Born in Vinebre, Spain, he became a priest and was the founder of a variety of apostolic associations for men, women, and children. He also founded the Society of St Teresa of Jesus to re-Christianize society through the Catholic education of women and children. See pages 132–33.

Bd Henry Suso, c. 1295–1365: This mystic and visionary was born in Switzerland and became a Dominican at a very young age. His *Book of Eternal Wisdom* is one of the most influential treatises in mystical literature. See pages 19–20, 67–68, 130–32.

St Hilary of Poitiers, died c. 368: Born of noble pagan parents, he became bishop of his native Poitiers. For his campaign against Arianism, he was exiled to Phrygia. Eventually, he was allowed to return. He is a Doctor of the Church. See pages 133–34.

St Hildegard of Bingen, 1098–1179: The first of the great German mystics, she was a nun and a prior, a poet and a prophet, a physician and a political moralist. She is called the Sibyl of the Rhine. See pages 20–21, 134–36.

St Hippolytus, ?–c. 235: A Roman priest, he was an important theological writer. A one-time antipope, he was reconciled with the Church but exiled for his faith to Sardinia, where he died of ill treatment. See page 186.

St Ignatius of Antioch, ?–107: Bishop of Antioch, he was probably a disciple of St John the Evangelist. Sent to Rome to be put to death as a Christian, he wrote seven letters to various churches on the way. See pages 21, 187.

St Ignatius of Loyola, 1491–1556: A nobleman of Spain, he heard the call of God after being wounded in battle against the French. He founded the Society of Jesus, whose members are to be spiritual soldiers. His *Spiritual Exercises* continues to be a religious work of vast influence. See pages 21, 69–70, 136.

St Irenaeus of Sirmium, ?–304: Bishop of Sirmium, he was arrested during Diocletian's persecution and beheaded for refusing to sacrifice to the Roman gods. See pages 136, 187.

Ven. James Alberione, 1884–1971: In reaction to the social and religious confusion of the turn of the century, he founded the Society of St Paul and the Daughters of St Paul, and under his guidance these communities evolved into an international effort to use all forms of media to proclaim the gospel. See pages 70–71, 187–88.

St Jane Frances Frémyot de Chantal, 1572–1641: Born in Dijon, France, she married the Baron de Chantal, with whom she had four children. After his death, under the spiritual direction of St Francis de Sales, she founded the Visitation Nuns. The congregation welcomed widows and those in poor health and consequently met with strong opposition during her lifetime. See page 137.

Bd Jeanne Jugan, 1792–1879: Her life was changed forever when she carried a sightless invalid woman to her own bed to die. Known as Sister Mary of the Cross, she founded the Little Sisters of the Poor in France. See pages 71, 137.

St Jerome, c. 342–420: From Dalmatia, he led a varied life of study, solitude, activity, and travel, then retired to Bethlehem, where he rested and retranslated the Latin Bible, known as the Vulgate. He is a Doctor of the Church. See page 71.

St John Chrysostom, c. 347–407: Born at Antioch, he soon developed a great gift of eloquence, for which he was known as Chrysostom, 'Golden Mouth.' As Patriarch of Constantinople he preached untiringly and founded hospitals and homes for the sick and needy. Exiled twice for his plain speaking, he is a Doctor of the Church. See pages 22, 137–39, 188.

St John Eudes, 1601–1680: One of the greatest 'home missioners' of his century, he was distinguished for his fearlessness in attending victims of the plague. He also founded the Sisters of Our Lady of Charity of the Refuge, from whom sprang the Good Shepherd Nuns, and the Congregation of Jesus and Mary (the Eudists). See page 72.

St John Leonardi, ?–1609: He founded the Congregation of Clerks Regular of the Mother of God. See page 22.

Bd John Martin Moye, 1730–1793: A French priest of Lorraine, he founded the Sisters of Providence to help the poor. He also went as a missionary to China, where he founded the Chinese Virgins, a counterpart to the European order. See pages 22–23, 139–40.

Bd John Ri, ?–1839: A Korean lay martyr. See page 75.

St John Vianney, 1786–1859: Known as the Curé of Ars, he had the gifts of healing and hidden knowledge; hundreds of thousands of pilgrims flocked to his small village near Lyons, France, just to receive the sacrament of reconciliation from him. See page 140.

St John de Brébeuf, ?–1649: A Jesuit, he worked among the Native Americans for thirty-four years before the Iroquois tortured and killed him. See page 140.

St John of the Cross (John de Yepes), 1542–1591: Born in Old Castile, Spain, this Carmelite friar was selected by St Teresa of Ávila as the first member of the first friary of the reformed observance. Establishing this reform among the male Carmelites, he endured persecution, including imprisonment at Toledo. He is a Doctor of the Church for his supreme mysticism, and his writings include *The Ascent of Mount Carmel, The Dark Night of the Soul,* and *The Spiritual Canticle.* See pages 24–28, 73–75, 141–42.

St John of Damascus, c. 675–c. 749: Born in Damascus of Christian Arab family, he served as finance minister for the Muslim caliph. Resigning his post, he went to Jerusalem to enter the Byzantine monastery at Mar Saba. His most famous work is *The Fount of Knowledge.* He is a Doctor of the Church. See pages 24, 72–73, 142.

Ven. Leo John Dehon, 1843–1925: As a young priest in France, he became concerned about unjust working conditions and began preaching the Church's social teaching. He is the founder of the Priests of the Sacred Heart. See pages 142–44.

St Leo the Great, died 461: Pope Leo I's defence of the Catholic faith against heresy and his intervention with Attila the Hun and Genseric the Vandal raised the prestige of the Holy See to great heights. One of only three popes called 'the Great,' he is a Doctor of the Church. See page 144.

St Leonard, died 550: A French hermit who withdrew from the court of King Clovis I, Leonard (Lienard) founded Noblac monastery, which grew into the town of Saint-Leonard. See pages 75–76, 144–45.

St Louise de Marillac, 1591–1660: A wealthy widow at age thirty-four, under the direction of St Vincent de Paul she began to work among the sick and destitute in Paris. She founded and directed the Daughters of Charity to found and staff shelters for abandoned women, orphanages, and schools throughout France. See pages 76–77, 147–48.

St Louis Marie Grignion de Montfort, 1673–1716: He founded the first establishment of the Missionary Priests of Mary, and his book *True Devotion to the Blessed Virgin* is well known. His emotional sermons aroused much opposition, yet he was a very successful missionary in Brittany. See pages 28, 145–47, 189.

St Lucian of Antioch, ?–312: A scriptural scholar, he went to Nicomedia where he was imprisoned for the faith for nine years and was then martyred. See page 29.

St Macarius, fourth century: One of two Egyptian Desert Fathers of the same name to whom the Jesus Prayer is ascribed. See page 77.

St Madeleine Sophie Barat, 1779–1865: Born in Burgundy, France, she founded the Society of the Sacred Heart, to educate girls who were growing up without the Faith after the turmoil of the French Revolution. See pages 29, 148.

St Margaret Mary Alacoque, 1647–1690: A native of Burgundy, she joined the Visitation Order and received a number of revelations and visions, including Christ's command that a liturgical feast be kept in honour of his Sacred Heart. See pages 77–78, 148–49, 189.

Bd Maria Helena Stollenwerk, 1852–1900: Born in the Eifel Mountains of Germany, she cooperated with Bd Arnold Janssen in establishing the international community of Holy Spirit Mission Sisters and the cloistered branch of Perpetual Adoration. See pages 29, 149.

St Maria Soledad Torres Acosta, 1826–1887: Dedicating her life to nursing the poor and abandoned sick in their own homes, she founded the Congregation of the Sisters, Servants of Mary in Madrid in 1851. See pages 29–30, 78, 150.

Bd Mariam Baouardy, 1846–1878: Born in Galilee under supernatural circumstances, she entered the Carmel of Pau when she began to receive the stigmata. Her charisms included levitation, ecstatic trances, prophecy, and bilocation. She also experienced severe demonic temptations. See pages 30–31, 150.

St Marie-Madeleine Postel, 1756–1846: Born in Barfleur, France, she sheltered fugitive priests in her home during the French Revolution. Afterward, she founded the Sisters of the Christian Schools of Mercy. See page 151.

Bd Marie of the Incarnation (Marie Guyard), 1599–1672: The daughter of a baker in Tours, she married at seventeen, had a son, and was widowed two years later. At the age of thirty she joined the Ursulines, and ten years later went to Quebec to lay the cornerstone for the first Ursuline convent there. She compiled dictionaries in Algonquin and Iroquois, and she experienced mystical visions. See pages 31, 151.

St Marguerite d'Youville, 1701–1771: Born in Quebec, she became a widow with three children to support. She founded the Grey Nuns and directed the General Hospital in Montreal. See page 29.

Bd Mary Angela Truszkowska, 1825–1899: Born in Kalisz, Poland, she devoted herself to working for the poor and needy. She founded the Congregation of Sisters of St Felix of Cantalice. See pages 151–52.

Bd Mary Ann of Jesus de Paredes y Flores, the Lily of Quito, 1618–1645: When Ecuador was struck by a series of calamities—earthquakes, epidemics, and a volcano eruption—she offered herself as a propitiatory offering. The calamities stopped, and she was stricken at once with an unidentifiable, lingering sickness, from which she died two months later. See page 31.

Bd Mary of Providence, 1825–1871: Founder of the Helpers of the Holy Souls, she suffered much and died from cancer. See page 78.

St Mary Magdalene dei Pazzi, 1566–1607: Born of an illustrious Florentine family, she entered Carmel at age sixteen. Afflicted with disease, spiritual dryness, and the assaults of unseen powers, she became known for her extraordinary patience. See pages 41, 152.

St Maximilian Kolbe, 1894–1941: Born in Poland, he is a 'martyr of charity,' having volunteered to take the place of a fellow concentration camp inmate condemned to death by the Nazis at Auschwitz. See pages 31–32.

St Mechtilde, ?–c. 1300: A countess by birth, she left her home in Islebe, Upper Saxony, at the age of seven to join the Benedictine convent. She received extraordinary illuminations, from Jesus, the Blessed Virgin Mary, and the saints. See pages 32, 152.

St Methodius, died 847: A Sicilian of aristocratic birth, he built a monastery on the island of Chio as a retreat. But he was summoned to Constantinople by St Nicephorus. After years of persecution, Methodius was named Patriarch of Constantinople. See pages 32–34, 78–79, 189.

St Methodius of Olympus, ?–c. 311: Bishop of Olympus in Lycia, he was martyred for the faith. He is famous for his writings. See page 153.

St Nicholas of Flüe, 1417–1487: Married young, he had ten children, but he left his family, with their consent, when he was fifty to spend the rest of his life as a hermit at Ranft. It is possible that he helped draw up the Edict of Stans when the Swiss Confederation was convulsed with dissensions. See page 153.

St Odo of Cluny, c. 879–942: One of the greatest abbots of Cluny, he dedicated his life to the reform of the monasteries in France. See page 153.

St Paschal Baylon, 1540–1592: Born in Aragon, he was a shepherd until becoming a lay-brother of the Alcantarine reform of the Friars Minor. Because of his devotion to the Blessed Sacrament and his defence of eucharistic doctrine before a Calvinist mob, he was declared the Patron of Eucharistic Congresses. See page 34.

St Patrick, c. 389–c. 461: A Romano-Briton, he was carried off as a slave to Ireland but escaped after six years. Having been consecrated a bishop, he returned to Ireland to take up missionary work and convert the Irish to Catholicism. See pages 153–56.

Bd Paul Giustiniani, 1476–1528: Born in Venice of a noble family, he entered the hermitage of Camaldoli after many years of humanist study. Ten years later, seeking a more solitary, austere life, he founded a religious family today known as the Camaldolese Hermits of Monte Corona. See page 157.

St Paul of the Cross, 1694–1775: Endowed with the gifts of prophecy and healing, he founded the Barefooted Clerks of the Cross and Passion (the Passionists). See page 189.

Bd Pauline von Mallinckrodt, 1817–1881: Born in Minden, Westphalia, the oldest daughter of the vice president, she worked to care for the neglected children of Paderborn, especially the blind. She founded the Congregation of the Sisters of Christian Charity in 1849, which opened schools, orphanages, and hospitals throughout Germany and North America. See pages 34–35, 157–60, 189.

St Paulinus of Aquileia, c. 726–804: Greatly respected by Charlemagne, he was made bishop of Aquileia. He was important in refuting the Adoptionist heresy then being spread in Spain. See page 35.

St Paulinus of Nola, c. 354–431: Born into a patrician family at Bordeaux, France, he was converted to Christianity by his Spanish wife and St Delphinus of Bordeaux. He was ordained and retired to Nola in Italy, where he built churches and was made bishop. See page 160.

St Peter Canisius, 1521–1597: Born at Nijmegen, he joined the Society of Jesus and devoted his energy to rebuilding the Church after the Reformation. He is a Doctor of the Church. See page 161.

St Peter Damian, 1007–1072: He was born an unwanted child in Ravenna and was ill treated until sent to school by a brother. He joined the hermit monks of Fonte Avellana and became abbot. Later, he was made cardinal-bishop of Ostia. He devoted his time to writing, preaching, and working against clerical abuses. He is a Doctor of the Church. See page 79.

St Peter of Alcantara, 1499–1562: A Franciscan of a reformed branch of the order, he began a yet more severe reform, whose members were referred to as Alcantarines. He was one of the great Spanish mystics of his time. See pages 35, 161–62.

PERMISSIONS, ACKNOWLEDGMENTS, AND SOURCES

Every effort has been made to locate and secure permission for the inclusion of all copyrighted material in this book. If any such acknowledgments have been inadvertently omitted, the publisher would appreciate receiving full information so that proper credit may be given in future editions.

The compiler wishes to express his gratitude as follows for permission to reproduce copyrighted materials:

The prayers of St Aelred of Rievaulx, 'Let your voice sound in my ears,' 'Thank you, good Jesus,' and 'Behold the wounds of my soul,' from *For Crist Luve: Prayers of Saint Aelred, Abbot of Rievaulx,* trans. by Sr. Rose de Lima, copyright © 1965 by Martinus Nijhoff, Den Haag, are reprinted with kind permission from Kluwer Academic Publishers, Spuiboulevard 50, P.O. Box 17, 3300 AA Dordrecht, The Netherlands.

The prayers of St Aelred of Rievaulx, 'God of mercy, hear the prayer that I offer'; St Birgitta, 'Eternal praise to you, my Lord Jesus Christ'; St Clement of Rome, 'Grant to us, Lord, that we may set our hope'; and St Odo of Cluny are from *Through the Year with the Saints: A Daily Companion for*

Private of Liturgical Prayer by M. Basil Pennington, OCSO. Copyright © 1988 by the Cistercian Abbey of Spencer, Inc. Used by permission of Doubleday, a division of Bantam Doubleday Dell Publishing Group, Inc.

The prayers of Sts. Afra, Agatha, Boris of Kiev, Clement of Rome, Crispina, Cyprian of Carthage, Dativus, Euplus, Ferreolus of Vienne, Ignatius of Antioch, Irenaeus of Sirmium, John Ri, Lucian of Antioch, Methodius of Olympus, Quirinus, Saturninus, Serenus, Theodata of Philippopolis, Theodotus of Ancyra, and Thomas Becket are taken from *Prayers of the Martyrs* by Duane W. H. Arnold. Copyright © 1991 by Duane W H Arnold. Used by permission of Zondervan Publishing House.

The prayers of Bd Aloysius Guanella are reprinted from *Nel mese del fervore,* courtesy Daughters of St Mary of Providence, Mount St Joseph, 24955 N. Highway 12, Lake Zurich, IL 60047-9752.

The prayers of Sts. Anselm of Canterbury, 'O merciful almighty Father,' 'We love you, O God,' and 'O blessed Lord, you have commanded us'; Basil the Great, 'O Lord our God, teach us'; Benedict, 'O Lord, I place myself in your hands'; Bernard of Clairvaux, 'Jesus! How sweet is the very thought of you'; Bernardine of Siena, 'Jesus, name full of glory'; Cyril; Edmund Rich of Abingdon; Francis Xavier, 'O my Lord Jesus!' and 'O God, you are the object of my love'; Gregory Nazianzen, 'Lord and Creator of all'; Gregory the Great, 'Look down, O Sovereign Creator'; Hippolytus; John de Brébeuf; John Eudes; John Leonardi; John Vianney; Macarius; Paschal Baylon; Paul of the Cross; Paulinus of Aquileia; Peter Canisius; Peter Damian; Pius X; and Bd Claude de la Colombière and Bd Crescentia Höss are from *Prayer Book of the Saints* comp. and ed. by Rev. Charles Dollen. Reprinted by permission of Fr. Dollen.

The excerpt from *St Anthony of Padua: Wisdom for Today* by Patrick McCloskey, O.F.M., copyright © 1977 by St Anthony Messenger Press, is reprinted by permission of the publisher. All rights reserved.

The prayer of St Anthony Mary Claret, 'O Jesus and Mary, the love I have for you,' from *Autobiography of Blessed Anthony Mary Claret,* trans. Louis Joseph Moore, C.M.F., is reprinted by permission of Claretian Missionaries, 1119 Westchester Place, Los Angeles, CA 90019.

The prayers of St Anthony Mary Claret, 'Father, give me humility' and 'Come, then, Lord, sustain your people,' are reprinted from his *Autobiography,* edited by José Maria Viñas, copyright © 1976 by Claretian Publications. Reprinted with permission from Claretian Publications, 205 W. Monroe Street, Chicago, IL 60606.

The prayers of Bd Arnold Janssen and Bd Maria Helena Stollenwerk are reprinted courtesy Arnold Janssen Spirituality Centre, Missiehuis St Michael, St Michaelstraat 7, 5935 BL Steyl, Netherlands.

The prayers of St Basil the Great, 'O Christ, our Master and God…' and 'O Christ our God, in all times….,' are reprinted courtesy Sisters of St Basil the Great, 710 Fox Chase Road, Fox Chase Manor, PA 19046-4198.

The prayer of St Bernadette, 'O Jesus, give me, I pray,' is reprinted courtesy Sisters of Nevers, 58000 St-Gildard, Nevers, France.

The prayers of St Bernardine of Siena, 'O Lord Jesus, acknowledge what is yours in us,' St Fulgentius, and St Venantius, from *Short Prayers for the Long Day* compiled by Giles and Melville Harcourt, copyright © 1978 by Giles and Melville Harcourt, are published with permission of Liguori/Triumph, One Liguori Drive, Liguori, MO 63057.

The prayers of St Catherine of Genoa, from *The Life and Sayings of St Catherine of Genoa* translated by Paul Garvin, copyright © 1964 by Alba House, are reprinted by permission of the publisher.

The prayer of St Catherine of Siena, 'Holy Spirit, come into my heart,' is translated by J. Robert Fenili, C.Ss.R., from *The History of St Catherine of Siena and Her Companions,* Augusta Theodosia Drane. London: Longmans, Green, & Co., 1899.

The prayers of St Clement Maria Hofbauer, from *Preaching the Gospel Anew: St Clement Maria Hofbauer* by Josef Heinzmann, C.Ss.R., copyright © Kanisius Verlag, Postfach 1052, Avenue de Beauregard 3, CH-1701 Freiburg, Germany, and © 1998 by Liguori Publications, are reprinted with permission of the publishers.

The prayers of St Clement of Rome, 'O God, make us children of quietness'; St Columba, 'Be thou a bright flame before me'; and St Ignatius of Loyola, 'Teach us, good Lord, to serve you as you deserve,' from *A Year with the Saints* by Mark Waters, copyright © 1997 by Mark Waters, are reprinted with permission of Liguori Publications, One Liguori Drive, Liguori, MO 63057.

The prayer of St Dimitrii of Rostov is reprinted from *The Orthodox Way* by Bishop Kallistos Ware, by permisiion of Mowbray & Co. Ltd.

The prayers of Bd Edith Stein, 'Seven Beams from a Pentecost Novena' and 'To God the Father' from *Edith Stein: Selected Writings,* trans. by Susanne M. Batzdorff, copyright © 1990 by Templegate Publishers, are reprinted with permission of the publisher.

The prayers of St Elizabeth Ann Bayley Seton are reprinted courtesy Sisters of Charity of New York, Mount St Vincent-on-Hudson, 6301 Riverdale Ave., Bronx, NY 10471.

The prayers of Bd Elizabeth of the Trinity, from *The Complete Works of Elizabeth of the Trinity,* vol. 1, translated by Sr. Aletheia Kane, O.C.D., copyright © 1984 by Washington Province of Discalced Carmelites, Inc., are reprinted with the permission of ICS Publications, 2131 Lincoln Rd. N.E., Washington, D.C. All rights reserved.

The prayers of St Ephrem the Syrian, 'Hymn IV,' 'Hymn V,' 'Hymn VII,' 'Hymn IX,' 'Hymn XIV' (pp. 101, 107–8, 130, 146–47, 181) from *Hymns on Paradise*, trans. by Sebastian Brock, copyright © 1990 by St Vladimir's Seminary Press, 575 Scarsdale Road, Crestwood, NY 10707, are reprinted with the permission of the publisher.

The prayers of St Frances Cabrini are reprinted courtesy MSC Word Ministry, 434 W. Deming Place, Chicago, IL 60614-1719.

The prayers of Ven. Francis Libermann are reprinted courtesy Congregation of the Holy Ghost, 6230 Brush Run Road, Bethal Park, PA 15102.

The prayers of St Gemma Galgani, from Germanus, Father, *Blessed Gemma Galgani: The Holy Maid of Lucca,* trans. Rev. A. M. O'Sullivan, O.S.B., copyright © 1933 by B. Herder Book Co., St Louis, are reprinted with permission of Burns & Oates, Tunbridge Wells, Kent, England.

The prayers of Bd George Matulaitis are reprinted courtesy Congregation of the Marian Fathers, American Province of Saint Casimir, 6336 S. Kilbourn Ave., Chicago, IL 60629-5588.

The prayers of Bd Henry Suso, from *The Soul's Love-Book* and *Little Book of Eternal Wisdom* as found in *The Exemplar: Life and Writings of Blessed Henry Suso, O.P.,* are reprinted with permission of The Priory Press, 7200 Division Street, River Forest, IL 60305.

The prayers of St Henry de Osso are reprinted courtesy Society of St Teresa of Jesus, 18080 St Joseph Way, Covington, LA 70435-5623.

The prayers of St Hildegard of Bingen are reprinted from St Hildegard of Bingen. *Symphonia: A Critical Edition of the Symphonia armonie celestium revelationum.* ed. and trans. by Barbara Newman. Copyright © 1989 by Cornell University Press. Used by permission of the publisher, Cornell University Press.

The prayers of St Ignatius of Loyola, 'Here I am, O supreme King and Lord of all things' and 'Take, Lord, all my freedom,' from *The Spiritual Exercises of St Ignatius,* trans. by Pierre Wolff, copyright © 1997 by Pierre Wolff, are reprinted with permission of Liguori/Triumph, Liguori Publications, One Liguori Drive, Liguori, MO 63057.

The prayer of Ven. James Alberione, 'May you be praised, Lord God, for the printed word…,' is reprinted courtesy Pauline Books and Media, 50 St Paul's Avenue, Boston, MA 02130.

The prayer of Ven. James Alberione, 'Father, in union with all those who celebrate the Eucharist…,' is reprinted courtesy Society of St Paul, P.O. Box 139, Ellsworth, OH 44416-0139.

The prayers of Bd Jeanne Jugan are reprinted courtesy Little Sisters of the Poor, Publications Office, 601 Maiden Choice Lane, Baltimore, MD 21228-3698.

The prayers of Bd John Martin Moye are reprinted from *Directory of the Sisters of Providence,* courtesy Congregation of Divine Providence, St Anne Convent, Melbourne, KY 41059.

The prayers of Ven. Leo John Dehon, SCJ, are from *Community Prayers of the Priests of the Sacred Heart,* trans. from *Thesaurus precum* of 1954; *The Life and Love Towards the Sacred Heart of Jesus,* trans. M. Jocelyn, 1945; and *Manuscrits divers,* as cited in *Etudes Dehoniennes,* vol. 2 (1966). All copyright Priests of the Sacred Heart, Hales Corners, WI. Reprinted by permission. All rights reserved.

The prayers of St Louis Marie Grignion de Montfort, from *God Alone: The Collected Writings of St Louis Mary de Montfort,* copyright © 1987 by Montfort Publications, 26 South Saxon Ave., Bay Shore, NY 11706-8993, are reprinted by permission of the publisher. All rights reserved.

The prayers of Bd Mariam Baouardy, from Brunot, Amedée, S.C.J., *Mariam: The Little Arab,* trans. Jeanne Dumais, O.C.D.S. and Sr. Miriam of Jesus, O.C.D., copyright © 1990, are reprinted with permission of The Carmel of Maria Regina, 87609 Green Hill Road, Eugene, OR 97402.

The prayers of St Marie-Madeleine Postel, from *Sainte Marie-Madeleine Postel* by His Lordship Mgr. Grente, Bishop of Le Mans, trans. by Katharine Henvey, London: Burns Oates & Washbourne Ltd., 1928, are reprinted by permission of the publisher.

The prayer of Bd Mary Angela Truszkowska is reprinted courtesy Congregation of Sisters of St Felix of Cantalice, via del Casaletto, 540, 00151 Rome, Italy.

The prayer of Bd Mary of Providence is reprinted courtesy Society of Helpers, 303 Barry Avenue, Chicago, IL 60657.

The prayer of St Maximilian Kolbe, from *Stronger than Hatred: A Collection of Spiritual Writings,* copyright © 1988 by New City Press, is reprinted by permission of the publisher and of the Curia Generalizia dei Frati Minori Conventuali, Piazza Ss. Apostoli, 51, 00187 Roma, Italy. All rights reserved.

The prayers of St Maria Soledad Torres Acosta are reprinted courtesy Sisters Servants of Mary, 800 North Eighteenth Street, Kansas City, KS 66102.

The prayers of Bd Marie of the Incarnation, from *Marie of the Incarnation: Selected Writings,* ed. Irene Mahoney, O.S.U., copyright © 1989 by Paulist Press, 997 Macarthur Boulevard, Mahwah, NJ 07430, are reprinted with permission of the publisher.

The prayer of Bd Paul Guistiniani, 'Lord, I know that what I have tried to say…,' is reprinted courtesy Holy Family Hermitage, Rt. 2, Box 36, Bloomingdale, OH 43910.

The prayers of Bd Pauline von Mallinckrodt are trans. by Sr. Floriana Cavlowicak, S.C.C., and reprinted courtesy Sisters of Christian Charity, 350 Bernardsville Road, Mendham, NJ 07945-0800.

The prayers of St Philip Neri are reprinted courtesy The Oratory, 434 Charlotte Ave., P.O. Box 11586, Rock Hill, SC 29731-1586.

The prayer of St Symeon 'You, O Christ, are the Kingdom of heaven,' is reprinted by permission of St Vladimir's Seminary Press, 575 Scarsdale Rd., Crestwood, NY 10707.

The prayer of Mother Teresa of Calcutta, from *Mother Teresa: In My Own Words,* ed. by José Luis González-Balado, copyright 1996 by José Luis González-Balado, is reprinted with permission of Liguori Publications, One Liguori Drive, Liguori, MO 63057.

The prayers of St Thomas Aquinas are reprinted courtesy Racine Dominican Archives, 5635 Erie Street, Racine, WI 53402-1900.

Other Sources

A Manual of Prayers for the Use of the Catholic Laity, Third Plenary Council of Baltimore, 1889.

Alphonsus de' Liguori, St *How to Face Death without Fear* ed. by Norman Muckerman, C.Ss.R. Liguori, Mo: Liguori Publications, 1976.

———. *Lord of My Heart.* ed. by Thomas Santa, C.Ss.R. Liguori, Mo.: Liguori Publications, 1997.

———. *Love God and Do What You Please.* adapted by M. J. Huber. Liguori, Mo.: Liguori Publications, 1970.

———. *Love Is Prayer, Prayer Is Love.* adapted by John Steingraeber, C.Ss.R. Liguori, Mo.: Liguori Publications, 1973.

———. *Meditations on the Eucharist.* ed. by Thomas Santa, C.Ss.R. Liguori, Mo.: Liguori Publications, 1997.

———. *Prayers Before and After Holy Communion.* adapted by H. J. O'Connell, C.Ss.R. Liguori, Mo.: Liguorian Pamphlets, 1962.

———. *Praying to God As a Friend.* Liguori, Mo.: Liguori Publications, 1987.

———. *Selected Writings and Prayers of St Alphonsus.* adapted by John Steingraeber, C.Ss.R. Liguori, Mo.: Liguori Publications, 1997.

Augustine, St *Confessions,* trans. by Edward B. Pusey. New York: P F Collier & Son, 1909.

Bernadette of Lourdes: The Only Complete Account of Her Life Ever Published. trans. J. H. Gregory. New York: Louché, Keane & Fitch, 1915.

Birgitta, St *Revelations of St Bridget, on the Life and Passion of Our Lord, and the Life of His Blessed Mother.* Fresno, Ca.: Academy Library Guild, 1957.

Boero, Joseph, S.J. *The Life of the Blessed Mary Ann of Jesus de Paredes y Flores, An American Virgin, Called the Lily of Quito.* Philadelphia: Peter F. Cunningham & Son, 1882.

Capes, Mary Reginald, O.S.D. *Richard of Wyche: Labourer, Scholar, Bishop, and Saint.* St Louis: B. Herder, 1913.

Drane, Augusta Theodosia. *The History of St Catherine of Siena and Her Companions.* London: Longmans, Green, & Co., 1899.

Ephrem the Syrian, St 'And since it is not profitable for us,' 'Before my offences,' and 'O Lord, we entreat of your goodness' in *Select Metrical Hymns and Homilies of Ephraem Syrus.* trans. Rev. Henry Burgess, Ph.D. London: Robert B. Blackader, 1853.

Fitts, Mary Pauline, G.N.S.H. *Hands to the Needy*. Garden City, N.Y.: Doubleday & Co., Inc., 1971.

Francis of Assisi, St 'Canticle of the Sun,' 'First Rule of the Friars Minor,' 'Letter to All the Friars,' 'Praises,' 'Praises of God,' and 'The Testament' in *The Writings of St Francis of Assisi*. trans. Father Paschal Robinson, Philadelphia: Dolphin Press, 1906.

Galilea, Segundo. *In Weakness, Strength*. Chicago: MSC Word Ministry, 1996.

Hage, Hyacinth, C.P. *The Life of Blessed Gabriel of Our Lady of Sorrows: Gabriel Possenti of the Congregation of the Passion*. rewritten and enlarged by Nicholas Ward, C.P. Philadelphia: H. L. Kilner & Co., 1910.

Hollings, Michael, and Etta Gullick, eds. *The One Who Listens: A Book of Prayer.* New York: Morehouse-Barlow Co., 1971.

Hopkins, Gerard Manley. *The Poems of Gerard Manley Hopkins*, ed. by W. H. Gardner and N. H. MacKenzie. London: Oxford University Press, 1967.

Houston, James M., ed. *The Love of God and Spiritual Friendship*. Sisters, Ore.: Multnomah Press, 1983.

John Chrysostom, St The Liturgy of Saint Chrysostom in *The Liturgies of SS. Mark, James, Clement, Chrysostom, and Basil,* trans. by Rev. J. M. Neale, D.D., and Rev. R. F. Littledale, LL.D. London: J. T. Hayes, 1869.

John of the Cross, St 'A Soul Longing for the Vision of God,' 'Mi Dios Y Mi Señor, Tened Memoria,' and 'Prayer of the Enamoured Soul' in *The Living Flame of Love*. trans. David Lewis. London: Thomas Baker, 1919.

————. *A Spiritual Canticle of the Soul*. trans. David Lewis. London: Thomas Baker, 1909.

Larssen, Raymond E. F, comp. and ed. *Saints at Prayer.* New York: Coward-McCann, Inc. 1942.

Lee, Rev. Frederick George. *The Christian Doctrine of Prayer for the Departed*. London: Daldy, Isbister, & Co., 1875.

Life of Blessed Madeleine Sophie Barat. Roehampton: 1911.

Lovat, Alice Lady. *Life of the Venerable Louise de Marillac*. New York: Longmans, Green & Co., 1916.

Miller, Louis, C.Ss.R. *Beacons of Light*. Liguori, Mo.: Liguori Publications, 1995.

More, St Thomas. *The Wisdom and Wit of Blessed Thomas More,* ed. by T. E. Bridgett, C.Ss.R. New York: Catholic Publication Society Co., 1892.

Patrick, St The Hymn, or 'Breastplate,' in *The Writings of St Patrick, the Apostle of Ireland,* 3d ed. revised trans. by Rev. Charles H. H. Wright, D.D. London: Religious Tract Society, 1894.

Peers, E. Allison, M.A. *Ramon Lull: A Biography*. London: Society for Promoting Christian Knowledge, 1929.

Puccini, Vincentio. *The Life of the Holy and Venerable Mother Suor Maria Maddalena de Patsi*. 1619.

Shepherd, Massey H., Jr., ed. *A Companion of Prayer for Daily Living*. Wilton, Conn.: Morehouse-Barlow Co., 1978.

Sicardo, Joseph, O.S.A. *Life of Sister St Rita of Cascia.* trans. by Dan J. Murphy, O.S.A. Philadelphia: H. L. Kilner & Co., 1916.

Soulier, Rev. Peregrine. *Life of Saint Philip Benizi of the Order of the Servants of Mary.* New York: Catholic Publication Society, 1886.

Southwell, Robert, St 'Hundredth Meditation' in *One Hundred Meditations on the Love of God.* ed. by John Morris. London: Burns and Oates, 1873.

――――. *Saint Peter's Complaint.* 1616.

――――. *St Mary Magdalens Tears.* 1616.

St John, Ambrose. *The Raccolta,* 10th ed. London: Burns Oates & Washbourne, Ltd., 1924.

The Revelations of St Gertrude. London: Burns Oates & Washbourne Ltd., 1870.

Thérèse of Lisieux, St *Histoire d'une Ame* ch. viii in *Thoughts of the Servant of God: Thérèse of the Child Jesus,* Dublin: Carmel of Kilmacud, 1914.

Ulanov, Barry, comp. *On Death: Wisdom and Consolation from the World's Great Writers.* Liguori, Mo.: Liguori/Triumph, 1996.

Van de Weyer, Robert. *The HarperCollins Book of Prayers.* San Francisco: HarperSan Francisco, 1993.

INDEX OF FIRST LINES

ABOUT THE COMPILER

Managing editor of the trade programme at Liguori Publications, Anthony F. Chiffolo has a master's degree in the classics of Western Civilization from St John's College in Annapolis, Maryland.